Revise Modern World History for AQA

Specification B

Alan Mendum
Steve Waugh

Heinemann

Heinemann Educational Publishers
Halley Court, Jordan Hill, Oxford OX2 8EJ
a division of Reed Educational & Professional Publishing Ltd
Heinemann is a registered trademark of Reed Educational &
Professional Publishing Ltd

OXFORD MELBOURNE AUCKLAND
JOHANNESBURG BLANTYRE GABORONE
IBADAN PORTSMOUTH NH (USA) CHICAGO

First published 2001

ISBN 0 435 31203 0

04 03 02 01
10 9 8 7 6 5 4 3 2 1

Designed, illustrated and typeset by Tech Set Ltd, Gateshead

Printed and bound in UK by Bath Press

Photographic acknowledgements
The authors and publisher would like to thank the following for permission to
reproduce photographs:

Associated Newspaper: 82
Bildarchiv Preußischer Kulturbesitz, Berlin: 133 (both)
Culver Pictures: 147
Hulton Getty: 95, 159
John Frost Newspaper Library: 64
National Army Museum: 58
Süddeutscher Verlag, Bilderdienst Munchen: 123 (left)

Cover photograph: © Thomas Hart Benton/Hulton Getty

Contents

Introduction

What do I study in Modern World History for AQA?

The Modern World History for GCSE course is one of three courses studied at GCSE. (The others are Schools History Project and British Social and Economic History.)

AQA

Paper 1: 1 hour 45 minutes
Questions on Conflict in the Modern World: International and British History
In Section A you must study one of three options, V, W or X on International History 1900-91.
You will be expected to answer two questions out of three on your chosen option. The questions will test your ability to recall, describe, analyse and explain factual information, as well as your ability to evaluate and analyse historical sources.
In Section B you must study one of two options, Y or Z, on British History.
You must answer one question on your chosen option. Questions will test your ability to recall, describe, analyse and explain factual information, to use historical sources, as well as to evaluate and interpret how events or people in the past have been represented in different ways.

Paper 2: 1 hour 45 minutes
Questions on Governments in Action
Russia/the USSR, 1914-41
Germany, 1918-39
The USA, 1919-41
Britain, 1905-51
You will be expected to answer questions on two of these Depth Studies. The questions will test your ability to interpret sources and representations, as well as to recall, describe, analyse and explain factual information.

Coursework/Paper 3
You can choose to do coursework or answer questions in Paper 3 (1 hour 30 minutes). You will be expected to do either two pieces of coursework, or to answer two exam questions, one of which must (normally) be on British History. Topics for coursework or Paper 3 will be additional to the content specified for Papers 1 and 2.

In each section you will find:

Topic summary

Sometimes studying history in depth can be confusing because you get to know so much detail that you lose sight of the 'big picture'. So we start each section with a summary of what the topic is about.

What do I need to know?

The revision guide then gives you a summary of what you need to know for the exam. Summary boxes are also included to give you a handy visual summary. When you have completed your revision you should be able to take a summary box and write at length about each point that is shown in it.

History of the topic

Here we give you the basic facts about the topic, but not in the same details as in your textbook and notes. We are not telling you the whole story again, but instead are summarising it to make it easier for you to learn.

What do I know?

Once you have completed your revision you might like to test yourself to see how much you know. We have included short self-assessment sections so that you can see just how thorough your revision has been. Most of the questions can be answered from information given in the summary, but we also presume that you have been learning the information in your book and notes!

Exam type question

You may be studying history because you love it and not care about how you do in the exam. For most students, however, what they really want is to do as well as possible in the examination. So we have given you lots of examples of the types of questions you will be asked together with some student answers.

Examiner's comments

The author of this book is an experienced teacher for this syllabus and he has commented on each exam question answer. By reading his comments you will be able to see what is good and what is disappointing in the answer. Then you can make sure that any answer you give in the exam is much better.

1 International History 1900–91

1.1 The causes of the First World War, 1900–14

Topic Summary

This period saw increasing rivalry between the Great Powers caused by long-term rivalries, the arms race and the alliance system. Rivalry was further increased by a series of crises in the Balkans and Morocco. The assassination of the heir to the Austrian throne in June 1914 provided the final cause of major war.

What do I Need to Know?

You will need to know the reasons for the First World War, especially the long-term rivalries between the Great Powers, the importance of the arms race and alliance system, the crises of 1905–14 and the impact of the assassination at Sarajevo.

Increased tension in Europe, 1900–14

Great Power rivalries
There was increasing tension between the Great Powers in the years before 1914.

France vs Germany
The French desired revenge after the defeat of 1871 in which the newly created German Empire seized the French provinces of Alsace and Lorraine. Many in France were determined to regain these provinces.

Britain vs Germany
This rivalry emerged mainly because of the policies of the German Kaiser, Wilhelm II:

- **Political rivalry.** Wilhelm II was determined to build up a German Empire. This brought competition with the British who already had an empire covering nearly one-quarter of the world.
- **Economic rivalry.** German industry was fast becoming efficient and the highest producer of goods. Britain felt threatened by the growth of German industry.
- **Naval rivalry** (see page 7).

Austria-Hungary vs Serbia

Austria-Hungary was a large empire of many different peoples including many Serbs. Serbia, to the south of this empire, wanted to create an enlarged Serbian state which would include the Serbs of Austria as well as Bosnia and Herzegovina. Austria felt increasingly threatened by Serbia.

Austria-Hungary vs Russia

Russia was the protector of the Slav peoples, such as the Serbs, of south-east Europe and supported Serbian ambitions for a larger state. This, in turn, incensed the Austrians.

The alliance system

By 1907 Europe was divided into two rival alliance systems.

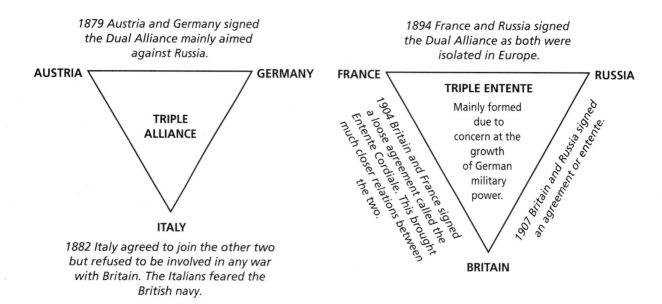

The alliance system brought war nearer: a quarrel between one member of each alliance system could well involve the other powers.

The arms race

There were three aspects to the arms race, each of which increased tension between the Great Powers:

- Competition in the size of armies.

- The development of weapons and build-up of armaments in each country.

- The naval race between Britain and Germany.

The naval race

In 1900 Britain had the largest and strongest navy in the world. Germany had the strongest army but the Kaiser decided to build a navy to compete with that of Britain.

- The launching of the Dreadnought in 1906 made all previous battleships obsolete and wiped out Britain's lead.

- Between 1906 and 1914, Britain built 29 Dreadnoughts; Germany built seventeen. This convinced the British that Germany intended to dominate Europe, if not the world.

The arms race aroused passions and the desire for war.

The crises of 1905–13

There were four major crises in this period each of which increased tension between the Great Powers and brought war one step nearer.

The Moroccan Crisis, 1905–6

- The French wished to make Morocco part of their North African Empire.

- The Kaiser hoped to split the Anglo-French entente and secure compensation from the French, in return for accepting the French occupation of Morocco.

- Britain backed France throughout and at the Algeciras Conference of 1906. This was a diplomatic defeat for the Kaiser who blamed the British for supporting France.

The Bosnian Crisis, 1908–9

- In 1908 Austria annexed (formally acquired) Bosnia and Herzegovina. This infuriated the Serbs who wanted these areas as part of a greater Serbia. Serbia, supported by Russia, protested, but Austria, supported by Germany, refused to back down and agree to a conference.

- The crisis increased rivalry between Austria, on the one side, and Serbia and Russia on the other.

The Agadir Crisis, 1911

- By 1911 it was obvious that France would finally occupy Morocco. The Kaiser sent a gunboat, *The Panther*, to the Moroccan port of Agadir to force compensation from France.

- Britain feared that Germany was trying to set up a naval base at Agadir and fully supported the French.

- The Kaiser was forced to scale down his demands. Again he blamed the British. Britain and France drew closer together.

3

The assassination at Sarajevo and the outbreak of war, 1914

The assassination

- On 28 June Austria's Archduke Franz-Ferdinand, the heir to the Austrian throne, was visiting the Bosnian capital, Sarajevo. He was assassinated by Gavrilo Princip, a member of the Black Hand terrorist organisation which wanted Serbia to be free of Austria-Hungary.
- Austria-Hungary blamed the Serbian government for the assassination. Austria demanded the Serbs give in to a series of tough demands. Serbia was protected by Russia, but Austria believed it could get what it wanted because it had Germany's support.

4 Aug	German troops crossed into Belgium. Britain declared war on Germany.
3 Aug	Germany declared war on France.
1 Aug	When Russia did not reply, Germany declared war. France now mobilised its army.
31 July	Germany called on Russia to stop its war preparations.
30 July	Russia began to mobilise its armed forces.
28 July	Austria declared war on Serbia. Serbia then appealed to Russia for help.

▲ The steps to war.

The Schlieffen Plan

- When France and Russia became allies, German military leaders knew they would have to fight the next war on two fronts. This had to be avoided at all costs.
- So, Count Schlieffen devised a plan. Germany would invade France and defeat it within six weeks. Then it would deal with Russia, which, he envisaged, would take six weeks to mobilise its army.
- The plan had a major flaw. The German army had to go through Belgium to invade and defeat France. This meant that Germany would ignore Belgian neutrality, and this brought Britain into the war.

Why did Britain go to war in 1914?

- The immediate reason was the German invasion of Belgium. The Treaty of London of 1839, signed by the Great Powers, had guaranteed the neutrality of Belgium. Germany had broken this Treaty. The Kaiser said Britain had gone to war over a 'scrap of paper'.
- Rivalry with Germany, especially the naval race.
- Obligations to France. Britain and France had drawn much closer as a result of the two Moroccan crises.
- British fears of a German victory and dominance in Europe.

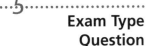

What do I Know?

Why did the following increase tension between the Great Powers:
- The alliance system
- The naval race
- The Schlieffen Plan?

1 Which provinces did Germany steal from France in 1871?
2 How did the Kaiser upset Britain in the years before 1914?
3 Which countries were the three members of the Triple Alliance?
4 What was the Triple Entente?
5 Which ship caused the naval race?
6 Why did the Kaiser interfere in Morocco in 1905?
7 Why did the gunboat, *The Panther*, cause a further crisis in Morocco?
8 Who shot Franz-Ferdinand?
9 Which country did Austria blame for the Archduke's murder?

My score ......

Exam Type Question

Here is the sort of source-based question you might be asked in an exam paper. Look closely at the answer given and the examiner's comments on it. Then answer the practice question.

Germany is deliberately preparing to destroy the British Empire. All of Europe is to be Germanised. We are all to be drilled and schooled and uniformed by German officials, and the Emperor William II is to rule us with a rod of iron. Britain alone stands in the way of Germany's path to world power and domination.

▲ From the *Daily Mail*, 1909.

How reliable is this source to an historian writing about Anglo-German relations in the years before the First World War? **(6 marks)**

Answer

I do not think this source would be reliable to an historian because it is written by a British newspaper which will be trying to convince the British public that it is Germany that is in the wrong. The reporter uses language and words which are very biased against Germany such as 'destroy the British Empire' and 'rule us with a rod of iron'. The reporter is stating opinions about German aims and not facts. Germany did want to build up its own empire and navy but there is little evidence that the Kaiser intended to destroy the British Empire and achieve the level of domination mentioned in the article. The article was written at the height of the Anglo-German naval race, when relations between the two countries were very strained and exaggerates German ambitions. It does, however, provide a reliable view of what many British people felt about the Germans in 1909.

Examiner's Comments

6 out of 6

This is a very strong answer because the student has judged the reliability of the source on its purpose, the situation in which it was written and the contents of the source. The answer uses references from the source itself to highlight its bias and stress its unreliability. The student remains focused on reliability all the way through the answer and does not make the mistake of simply describing what the source says.

6

Practice Question

Now try to answer this sort of question yourself.

> I no longer have any doubt that Britain, Russia and France have agreed among themselves to wage war to destroy us. The encirclement of Germany has already begun.

▲ **Kaiser Wilhelm II speaking in 1914 before the outbreak of the war.**

How reliable is this source to an historian writing about the rivalry between Germany and the members of the Triple Entente?

(6 marks)

Remember that to answer a question on reliability you need to look at the following points:

1 Who wrote/made the source? Do they have a reason to be biased?

2 In what situation was the source written or made? Are there any special circumstances which might affect the reliability of the source?

3 Why was the source made or written? Did the author/artist have a specific reason for saying this? How does this affect its reliability?

4 Reliability is about trust. Do any of the words or images suggest that you cannot trust the source?

5 Compare what the source shows or says with your own knowledge. Is it giving a reliable view or facts about the person or event?

1.2 How did the Treaty of Versailles establish peace?

......1......

Topic Summary

When the First World War ended the victorious powers met at Versailles to agree the peace terms that were to be imposed on the defeated nations. Unfortunately there was much opposition to the terms of the treaty, especially in Germany.

......2......

What do I Need to Know?

You will need to know the motives of the three Allied leaders at the Treaty of Versailles. You could well be asked about German reactions to this treaty and whether the terms imposed on Germany were fair.

......3......

The Treaty of Versailles

The Big Three

This was the name given to the three Allied leaders who met at Versailles to decide the peace terms. They had different and often conflicting aims.

Woodrow Wilson, US President

- The USA had joined the war only in April 1917. War damage was slight and casualties were low in comparison with France and Britain.

- Wilson believed Germany was to blame for the war but he believed that the Treaty should not be too harsh. One day Germany would recover and might want revenge.

- He based his ideas on the Fourteen Points, the most important of which was self-determination – the belief that people should rule themselves and not be ruled by a foreign power.

Georges Clemenceau, French Prime Minister

- During the war France had suffered enormous damage. Large areas of land had been devastated and many factories destroyed. Millions of French people had been killed. Clemenceau was under pressure from the French people to make Germany suffer.

- He was also anxious about the future. He did not want Germany to recover and be a threat to France.

Lloyd George, British Prime Minister

- People in Britain were bitter towards Germany. They wanted a harsh peace treaty and Lloyd George had promised them that Germany would be punished.
- However, he wanted Germany to be justly punished. Like Wilson he believed that Germany might want revenge in the future and could possibly start another war. He also wanted Britain and Germany to start trading with each other again.
- Lloyd George was often in the middle ground between Clemenceau and Wilson at the peace talks. He did not agree with Wilson's Fourteen Points, which he saw as too idealistic, but he didn't want to cripple Germany as much as Clemenceau did.

Summary box 1

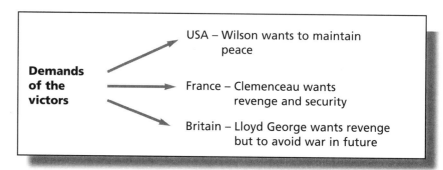

The Treaty of Versailles

Clemenceau was pleased with the Treaty of Versailles because Germany was firmly dealt with.

Military terms

German armed forces were reduced to well below the level they had been before the war:

- The army was limited to 100,000 and conscription was banned.
- Germany was not allowed armoured vehicles, submarines or aircraft.
- The navy could have only six battleships.
- To protect the French border a demilitarised zone 50 kilometres wide was established on the east bank of the Rhine.

War Guilt and reparations

- The Allies made Germany agree to Article 231 (the 'War Guilt' clause) which said that the war was Germany's fault.
- This gave the legal excuse for making the Germans pay reparations. The sum was set at £6600 million, to be paid in instalments over 42 years.
- These payments were demanded even though the German economy was in ruins after the War and the Treaty took German merchant ships and railway engines. Much of the land lost by Germany contained valuable coal and iron deposits which were now no longer available to the Germans.

Territorial losses

- All German colonies were taken and given to the victorious powers to govern (as mandates).
- German land was given to Belgium, France, Denmark and Poland with the League of Nations (see p. 16) looking after several ex-German cities. Alsace and Lorraine were returned to France; Eupen and Malmédy went to Belgium; North Schleswig went to Denmark. In all, Germany gave up 10 per cent of its land size. Most importantly, by giving West Prussia to Poland the peacemakers divided Germany into two.
- Germany lost all the land taken from Russia in the Treaty of Brest-Litovsk in 1918.
- Germany was forbidden to unite with Austria.

German reactions to the Treaty of Versailles

The Germans were shocked at the Treaty of Versailles and felt the terms were totally unfair and far too harsh.

- They were upset that they were not represented at the peace talks and that the Treaty was a 'diktat' (dictated peace) forced upon them.
- The Germans hated the War Guilt clause. At the very least they thought that other countries should share the blame for the War.
- The loss of territory was deeply resented. The Treaty went against Wilson's Fourteen Points, especially self-determination, by placing many Germans under foreign governments; for example, the Germans in the Sudetenland were under the control of Czechoslovakia. East Prussia was split from the rest of Germany by the Polish Corridor, the area taken from Germany and given to Poland.
- The war was followed by economic chaos and high inflation in Germany which the Germans blamed on having to pay reparations.
- The disarmament terms angered most Germans. The army was a symbol of German pride and was now far too small for a country of Germany's size.

Summary box 2

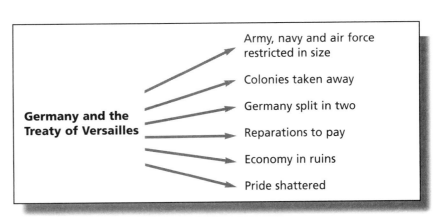

13

Was the treatment of Germany fair?

Whether or not the Treaty of Versailles was fair is a question historians have to decide for themselves. You need to make up your own mind, but just think about these points:

- At the time some people said it was too harsh on Germany and others that it did not punish Germany enough.
- What would Germany have done if it had won the war? In 1871 it had made France pay large sums of money and took Alsace and Lorraine. In March 1918 the Germans forced very harsh peace terms on the Russians at the Treaty of Brest-Litovsk.
- Could the Allies have just forgotten about what happened in the War and carried on as if nothing had happened? What would the people of France and Britain, whose compatriots had been killed, have thought of this?

4

What do I Know?

What differences were there between the aims of:

- Clemenceau
- Lloyd George
- Wilson

in the peace negotiation?

1 Who were the 'Big Three'?
2 What was self-determination?
3 After Versailles, what was the maximum size of the German army?
4 How much did Germany have to pay in reparations and for how many years?
5 What was the 'War Guilt' clause?
6 What happened to East Prussia?
7 Why was the Treaty of Versailles described as a 'diktat'?

My score ......

5

Exam Type Question

Here is the sort of source-based question you might be asked in an exam paper. Look closely at the answers given and the examiner's comments on them. Then answer the practice question.

> 25 March 1919. The great topic is Poland. David (Lloyd George) is dead against the 'corridor' system, under which a large slice of Germany containing 3 million Germans is lopped off and put under the Poles. David says it will simply mean another war. The French are furious with him for opposing the idea. David says the peace must be a just peace and we must prepare terms for the Germans to sign that we shall feel justified in insisting upon. To add this corridor to Poland is simply to create another Alsace-Lorraine.

▲ Extract from *Lloyd George: A Diary* by Frances Stevenson, secretary and close companion to Lloyd George.

How reliable is this source to an historian studying the peace negotiations leading to the Treaty of Versailles? **(6 marks)**

Answer 1

This is reliable because it was written at the time by someone who knew Lloyd George. It tells us about land being taken off Germany and given to Poland.

Answer 2

This is reliable in its views about the Polish Corridor. The Germans certainly were very upset by the loss of the area which split East Prussia from the rest of Germany. The source is less reliable about Lloyd George's motives and the attitude of France. She rightly points out that he wanted a fair and just treaty. He did not want Germany punished too much because this might lead to another war. The French were determined to punish Germany as much as possible. On the other hand, she fails to mention the pressures on Lloyd George from the British public who wanted to make Germany pay.

Examiner's Comments: Answer 1

1–2 out of 6

This is a very weak answer. It makes the simple assumption that the source is reliable because it was written at the time and then goes on to describe the source contents.

Answer 2

4–5 out of 6

This is a good answer which assess reliability on the contents of the source compared to the student's own knowledge. For example, the student focuses on the reliability of the conflict over the Polish Corridor and Lloyd George's motives. To achieve maximum marks I would expect some discussion of purpose, bias and/or situation related to reliability.

Practice Question

Now try to answer this sort of question yourself.

> I cannot feel President Wilson is to be blamed. I have seen day by day his struggle. But they have taken the heart out of the peace. We had such high hopes; and now, at the end, we are doing hell's work, starving people, grabbing territory – or helping to grab it for our friends – standing by while this grand gesture of revenge and humiliation is made.

▲ **An American journalist commenting in June 1919 on the Treaty of Versailles.**

How reliable is this source for an historian studying the Treaty of Versailles? **(6 marks)**

Look back on page 10 for tips on answering questions on reliability.

1.3 Why did the League of Nations frequently fail in its aims to keep peace?

1

Topic Summary

The peacemakers at Versailles also set up the League of Nations in the hope that an international organisation would maintain peace and prevent the outbreak of war. The League, however, had many weaknesses from the start and, although successful in resolving minor disputes, failed when confronted with major crises such as the Japanese invasion of Manchuria in 1931 and the Italian seizure of Abyssinia in 1935.

2

What do I Need to Know?

You will need to be aware of the aims, organisation and powers of the League of Nations. The most commonly asked question is why the League failed, so have a sound knowledge of its weaknesses and failures as well as the causes, events and results of the Manchurian and Abyssinian crises.

3

Failures of the League of Nations

Aims and organisation

In 1918 President Wilson had called for a 'general association of nations' to prevent further wars. This organisation was set up in the Treaty of Versailles. The League of Nations had a Covenant (set of rules) which laid out its aims. These were to:

- encourage co-operation between nations

- prevent aggression by any nation

- work towards international disarmament

- improve the working and living conditions of all people.

The League was built around the idea of collective security. This meant that its members could prevent war by acting together to protect and defend the interests of all nations. The League would settle disputes by:

- arbitration by a neutral country

- taking the matter to the International Court of Justice

- an inquiry by the Council (see page 17).

Summary box 1

The organisation of the League of Nations

Secretariat – to carry out the administration

Assembly – all nations to discuss international issues

Council – committee to discuss international issues

International Court of Justice – to settle international disputes

Weaknesses of the League of Nations
In theory the League was quite powerful:

- In 1920 it had 42 members. Eight years later this had risen to 60.
- There was a strong desire for peace and international disarmament – a determination to prevent another major war.
- The League could take action against an aggressor, including imposing economic sanctions (stopping members of the League trading with an aggressor) and military force.

However, these strengths were outweighed by its weaknesses.

Limited powers
- The League had no armed forces of its own. It relied entirely upon the co-operation of its members to carry out its decisions. They, however, were reluctant to use force against other nations and, in any case, disagreed over various issues, especially the treatment of Germany in the early 1920s.
- Military force would always be a last resort because of cost. Britain and France were still trying to recover from the economic effects of the First World War.
- Economic sanctions were difficult to enforce. Member countries were unwilling to stop trading with an aggressor because it could harm their own trade.
- The League could often force smaller nations to give way but was powerless to prevent aggression by more powerful countries.

Membership
Some important countries did not join the League:

- The USA never joined the League despite the wishes of Wilson. Many Americans wanted to keep the USA out of European political affairs.
- Bolshevik Russia was not allowed to join. Britain and France were suspicious of the Bolsheviks and feared the spread of communism to the West. The Bolsheviks saw the League of Nations as a club dominated by rich countries opposed to communism.
- The defeated nations, such as Germany and Austria, were not allowed to join.

The Manchurian Crisis, 1931

In 1931 Japan invaded the Chinese province of Manchuria. This was the first major test of the powers of the League of Nations but it failed to stop Japanese aggression.

Causes

There were several reasons for the Japanese aggression:

- Japan was a rising power in Asia and the Pacific and had very quickly developed into a modern trading nation.
- There were powerful groups in Japan (especially in the army) which wanted Japan to expand and build an empire.
- The Wall Street Crash of 1929 and the Depression had a major impact on the Japanese economy. Its trade was also badly affected. Japan began to look for other ways to expand.
- Japan was also short of living space for its population.
- Manchuria was rich in natural resources, such as iron ore and coal which Japanese industry needed.
- Japan claimed that the Manchurian railway, which it protected, was being attacked by Chinese troops.

Events

China appealed to the League of Nations for help.

- Early in 1932 the League set up a Commission under Lord Lytton. The Commission condemned the Japanese invasion.
- Japan carried on capturing parts of Manchuria which it had renamed Manchukuo, and left the League.
- The League took no further action. Britain did not want to provoke Japan in case it attacked her colonies in the Far East.
- In 1937 Japan launched attacks on other parts of China.

Effects

- Japan had captured Manchuria and had a base for future attacks on China.
- The League had been shown to be weak and not prepared to take action when the interests of its major members, for example Britain, were not at stake.
- This encouraged further aggression, especially from Italy and Germany.

Summary box 2

Japanese invasion of Manchuria

Why?	What happened?	Consequences
• Space for population	• Manchurian railway attacked	• Manchuria becomes Japanese possession
• Raw materials	• Japanese invasion	
• New markets	• Lytton Commission	• League appears weak
	• Japan leaves League	

The Abyssinian Crisis, 1935–36

In 1935 the Italian leader, Mussolini, decided to invade Abyssinia in Africa. He did this because:

- Italy already had possessions in Africa around Abyssinia.
- Mussolini wanted revenge for Abyssinia's defeat of Italy in the Battle of Adowa in 1896.
- Mussolini wanted to build a great Italian empire like the old Roman Empire.
- Abyssinian tribespeople had killed 30 Italian soldiers in a border skirmish at Wal-Wal in 1934.

The Italians invaded in October 1935, using modern weapons such as aircraft and poisonous gas, against which the Abyssinians had little defence. The Abyssinian leader, Haile Selassie, appealed to the League of Nations for help.

- The League decided that Italy was the aggressor.
- Economic sanctions were applied.

However:

- Coal, oil and steel were excluded from the sanctions.
- Not all countries applied sanctions.
- Britain and France did not stop Mussolini using the Suez Canal to reach Abyssinia.
- In December 1935 Britain and France proposed that Mussolini should get two-thirds of Abyssinia if he stopped fighting. This was known as the Hoare–Laval Pact. Britain and France wanted to keep Mussolini 'sweet' so he would not ally with Hitler. A public outcry in both countries forced the withdrawal of this Pact.
- Other nations now withdrew their sanctions.

Summary box 3

The Italian invasion of Abyssinia

Why?	What happened?	Consequences
Building an empire	Italian invasion with modern weapons	Abyssinia becomes an Italian possession
Revenge for Adowa	Haile Selassie appeals to League	League destroyed as an effective peace-keeping force
Attacks on Italians	League imposes sanctions	Mussolini leaves League
	Hoare–Laval Pact	Britain and France look to other ways to keep peace

Results of Abyssinian Crisis

- Abyssinia became an Italian possession.
- The League was totally discredited. Not only had it failed to act effectively, but its most powerful members had acted against it.

Why did the League of Nations fail?

There were several reasons:

- The self-interest of leading members. When conflicts occurred, neither the French nor British governments were prepared to abandon their own self-interests in support of the League.
- The USA and other important countries were absent. Germany was not a member until 1926 and left in 1933. The USSR did not join until 1934, while Japan left in 1933 and Italy left in 1937. The League therefore lacked real authority.
- Economic sanctions did not work; they were easily broken.
- Lack of armed forces. The League had no troops and Britain and France were unwilling to commit troops.
- The treaties it had to uphold were seen as unfair. The League was seen as an organisation run by the victorious to keep in place the unfair peace treaties of 1919–20.
- Decisions were slow. When a crisis occurred, the League was supposed to act quickly and with determination. In practice it was very difficult for members to agree on a course of action. Decisions were often made too late.

4

What do I Know?

What was the importance of the following:

- The organisation of the League of Nations
- League membership, 1920–35
- The Manchurian Crisis, 1931–33
- The Abyssinian Crisis, 1935?

1. What is meant by 'sanctions'?
2. Why did the USA not join the League of Nations?
3. Give one reason for the Japanese invasion of Manchuria in 1931.
4. What was the Lytton Commission?
5. Why did the Manchurian Crisis weaken the League of Nations?
6. Give one reason for Mussolini's invasion of Abyssinia in 1935.
7. What was the Hoare–Laval Pact?
8. Who was the Emperor of Abyssinia in 1935?
9. What effects did the Abyssinian Crisis have on the League of Nations?
10. Give two reasons for the failure of the League of Nations.

My score ......

5

Exam Type Question

Here is the sort of question you might be asked in an exam paper. Look closely at the answer given and the examiner's comments on it. Then answer the practice question.

> Describe the aims and organisation of the League of Nations.
>
> **(6 marks)**

Answer

The League of Nations aimed to maintain peace through collective security. It wanted to prevent aggression by any nation, work towards international disarmament and improve the living and working conditions of people.

The League had an Assembly, a Council, a Permanent Court of Justice and Special Committees.

Examiner's Comments

3 out of 6

The student has given a detailed explanation of the aims of the League. He or she has not explained the organisation of the League, simply mentioning the key bodies. In effect the question has been only half-answered.

6

Practice Question

Now try to answer this sort of question yourself.

Describe how the League of Nations acted during the Manchurian Crisis of 1931 and the Abyssinian Crisis of 1935–36.   **(6 marks)**

Remember that to answer this question you need to work along the following guidelines:

1 Give a detailed description of the factor or factors mentioned in the question. If there are two factors, explain each in detail.

2 Be precise in your description.

3 Write two good-length paragraphs because this question is worth 6 marks.

1.4 How did Hitler challenge the Treaty of Versailles, 1933–38?

1

Topic Summary

Adolf Hitler became Chancellor of Germany in January 1933. He was determined to overturn the Treaty of Versailles and expand Germany eastwards. Over the next few years he began a programme of rearmament, reoccupied the Rhineland and occupied Austria. There was little or no opposition from France and Britain.

2

What do I Need to Know?

You will need to know about Hitler's aims and ambitions, his rearmament policies of 1933-35 and the reoccupation of the Rhineland. In addition, you will need to understand his reasons for uniting with Austria and how this was achieved. You may be asked why Hitler was so successful during this period and, more especially, why Britain and France reacted to Hitler's demands in the way they did.

3

Hitler's challenge to the Treaty of Versailles

Hitler's aims

Hitler had several aims:

- He believed the Treaty of Versailles was the major cause of Germany's problems. He promised the German people that he would reverse the Treaty and get back the territory Germany had lost.
- He wanted to expand eastwards to create more *Lebensraum* (living space) for the German people. He was looking towards Czechoslovakia, Poland and the USSR. This followed from Hitler's belief in the supremacy of the Aryan race, the 'master race'. The Slavs of Eastern Europe - the Poles, Czechs and Russians - were seen as *Untermenschen* (subhumans).

To achieve these aims he needed to build up the German armed forces.

Hitler's policies 1933–36

- In 1931, 61 nations met at a conference to discuss disarmament. Hitler walked out of the conference when the other powers refused to disarm to Germany's level. This gave Hitler the legal justification to begin rearmament.
- From 1933 he began building a new air force, the *Luftwaffe*, and the following year announced conscription and a peacetime army of 550,000; all were breaches of the Treaty of Versailles.

- At first Britain, France and Italy made a united stand against Hitler and in 1935 met at Stresa to condemn his rearmament policies. However, this unity was destroyed when Britain agreed to sign a naval treaty with Germany. This allowed Germany to build a navy 35 per cent of the size of Britain's, as well as submarines. Britain was now officially accepting German rearmament and thus the end of the military terms of the Treaty of Versailles.
- In the same year, people in the coalmining area of the Saar, which had been placed under the control of the League of Nations, voted by 477,000 to 48,000 to return to German control.

The reoccupation of the Rhineland, 1936

In March 1936 German troops moved back to the Rhineland. This was a calculated risk by Hitler:

- It was a clear breach of the Treaty of Versailles.
- German troops were in no position to stand up to the French army if it reacted. Indeed, Hitler's troops were under strict orders to retreat if this happened.

However, there was no resistance because France was preoccupied with domestic problems and Britain was not keen to provoke Germany. Hitler's gamble paid off. This success convinced Hitler that Britain and France would not stop him achieving his aims.

The *Anschluss* (union) with Austria, 1938

Hitler had been born in Austria and one of his aims was to see Germany and Austria unite as one country. By 1938 Hitler was ready:

- Hitler bullied the Austrian Chancellor, Schuschnigg, into accepting a Nazi, Seyss-Inquart, as Minister of the Interior.
- Schuschnigg ordered a plebiscite (vote) to be held to find out if the people of Austria really wanted union with Germany.
- Hitler feared a 'no' vote, so he moved troops to the Austrian border, and threatened to invade if Schuschnigg did not resign in favour of Seyss-Inquart.
- Seyss-Inquart became Chancellor and invited German troops into Austria. On 12 March 1938 the German army entered Vienna.

Hitler had once again broken the Treaty of Versailles. Britain and France did nothing. This was because:

- Hitler was Austrian and many Austrian people welcomed the *Anschluss*. In the plebiscite over 99 per cent voted in favour of union with Germany.
- There was a feeling among people in Britain that the Treaty of Versailles had been harsh on Germany and Britain should not defend it.

Summary box 1

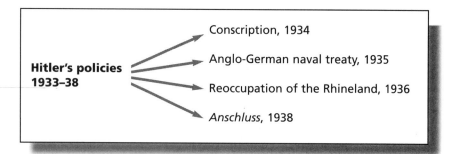

Hitler's policies 1933–38

Conscription, 1934

Anglo-German naval treaty, 1935

Reoccupation of the Rhineland, 1936

Anschluss, 1938

What do I Know?

Why did Britain and France do little or nothing to stop:

- German rearmament
- The reoccupation of the Rhineland
- The *Anschluss*?

1 What was meant by *Lebensraum*?
2 Why did Hitler walk out of the International Disarmament Conference?
3 When did Hitler introduce conscription?
4 Which coalmining area was returned to Germany in 1935?
5 Why was the reoccupation of the Rhineland by German troops a gamble in 1936?
6 Did the gamble work?
7 What was the *Anschluss*?
8 Who were Schuschnigg and Seyss-Inquart?

My score ......

1.5 Why did appeasement fail to prevent the outbreak of war in 1939?

Topic Summary

Hitler had not exhausted his ambitions with the occupation of the Rhineland. Instead he turned to Czechoslovakia and the area known as the Sudetenland. German threats to invade led to the Munich Conference at the end of September 1938. Hitler was given the Sudetenland but, despite promises to the contrary, German troops marched into the rest of Czechoslovakia in March 1939. Britain and France had tried unsuccessfully to appease Hitler but refused to give way to his next demands – access through the Polish Corridor to East Prussia. On 1 September German troops invaded Poland. Two days later Britain and France declared war on Germany.

What do I Need to Know?

You will need to know the meaning of appeasement as well as the arguments for and against this policy. Examiners may also ask for reasons for the outbreak of war in September 1939 together with details of the Czech Crisis of 1938 and the key events of 1939 including the Nazi–Soviet Non-Aggression Pact and the Polish Crisis.

The failure of appeasement

The Czech Crisis, 1938

- Hitler wanted to expand into the area of Czechoslovakia known as the Sudetenland. It consisted of 3 million German-speaking peoples.
- Hitler ordered Henlein, the leader of the Sudeten Germans, to stir up trouble in the Sudetenland and demand self-government and union with Germany.
- Hitler threatened to invade Czechoslovakia unless these demands were met.
- The British Prime Minister, Neville Chamberlain, believed a peaceful solution could be worked out. At first he persuaded the Czech President, Benes, to agree to self-government for the Sudetenland.
- On 29–30 September 1938, Hitler met Chamberlain, Mussolini and the French Prime Minister, Daladier, at Munich. The Czechs were not invited to the meeting in which they were forced to hand over the Sudetenland to Germany.
- In this meeting at Munich both men promised that Britain and Germany would not go to war. Hitler promised that he did not want the rest of Czechoslovakia.

Chamberlain returned to Britain a hero. He had prevented war, saying the agreement was 'Peace for our time'. The results of Munich, however, were serious for Czechoslovakia and Europe as a whole:

- The Czech government was completely humiliated.
- Czechoslovakia was now defenceless: the Sudetenland contained its defences against Germany.
- Britain and France had again shown their weakness by giving way to Germany.

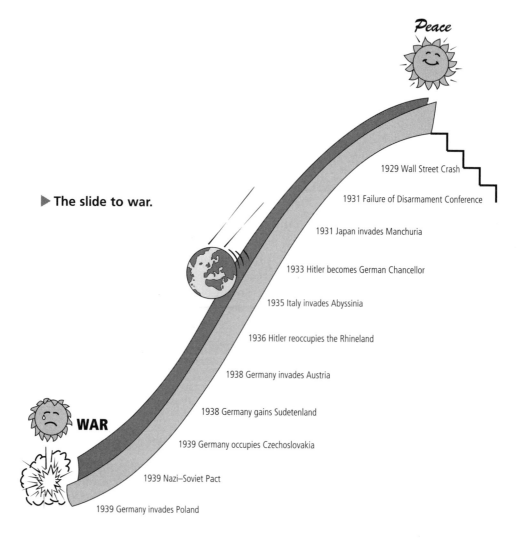

▶ **The slide to war.**

Peace

1929 Wall Street Crash
1931 Failure of Disarmament Conference
1931 Japan invades Manchuria
1933 Hitler becomes German Chancellor
1935 Italy invades Abyssinia
1936 Hitler reoccupies the Rhineland
1938 Germany invades Austria
1938 Germany gains Sudetenland
1939 Germany occupies Czechoslovakia
1939 Nazi–Soviet Pact
1939 Germany invades Poland

WAR

The events of 1939

- In March 1939 Hitler invaded what was left of Czechoslovakia.
- Britain and France now abandoned their policy of appeasement (see page 27) realising that Hitler's promises made at Munich were worthless. They were rapidly rearming and were determined to stand up to future German demands.

- Poland was Hitler's next target. In April Hitler demanded the return of the port of Danzig and the Polish Corridor. Britain and France signed an alliance with Poland; Poland refused Hitler's demands.
- The future of Poland now depended on the attitude of the Soviet Union. Britain and France reluctantly opened talks with Stalin, the Soviet leader, but were very surprised when the Nazi–Soviet Non-Aggression Pact was signed on 23 August 1939. This Pact guaranteed that the Soviets and Germans would not fight each other in the event of war in Europe. In secret both powers agreed to divide up Polish territory should war occur.
- On 1 September 1939 Hitler invaded Poland. He did not believe that Britain and France would go to war.
- On 3 September Britain and France declared war on Germany.

Appeasement

Britain and France followed this policy in the mid- and late 1930s. It meant giving Hitler what he wanted on condition that he did not try to expand further. The two countries did not want war as they felt they were not strong enough. However, at the same time Britain and France began to rearm.

In 1938 this policy appeared to be working, but by the end of 1939 it had been shown to be unsuccessful. Was the policy followed by Chamberlain justified? This is a question you will need to answer yourself, but here are some suggestions:

Against:

- Appeasement was morally wrong. If Hitler used 'bullying tactics' it was up to Britain to oppose him.
- By following appeasement Britain betrayed the Austrians and the Czechs.
- Appeasement made Britain look weak and gave Hitler the confidence to step up his demands.
- Appeasement did not work because Hitler could not be trusted to keep his word.

For:

- Britain was not ready to go to war and had to buy time to prepare.
- Germany was mistreated at Versailles and most of Hitler's demands were reasonable.
- War had to be avoided at all costs.
- Hitler was anti-communist and was doing a good job of restoring Germany, so he should be supported.
- By following the policy of appeasement Hitler was shown to be clearly in the wrong and a man not to be trusted, so the British people would not then hesitate to go to war.

4 What do I Know?

1. Why did Hitler demand the area known as the Sudetenland?
2. What was agreed at the Munich Conference in September 1938?
3. Which country was not invited to this conference?
4. How long did Hitler stick to the promises he made at Munich?
5. What did Hitler demand from Poland in April 1939?
6. What did Germany and the Soviet Union agree in the Pact of August 1939?
7. When did Hitler invade Poland?
8. Which two countries signed an alliance with Poland?
9. What was meant by the policy of appeasement?
10. When did Britain and France declare war on Germany?

My score ......

Give three reasons:
- Justifying the policy of appeasement
- Criticising this policy.

5 Exam Type Question

Here is the sort of causation question you might be asked in an exam paper. Look closely at the answers given and the examiner's comments on them. Then answer the practice question.

Was the failure of appeasement the most important reason for the outbreak of the Second World War? **(10 marks)**

Answer 1

I agree that it was the failure of appeasement which led to the outbreak of war. Appeasement was the policy carried out by Britain and France. They were prepared to give way to Hitler's demands in order to keep the peace. In 1938 they gave Hitler the Sudetenland to stop him invading Czechoslovakia. Hitler saw this as a sign of weakness and believed Britain and France would not go to war to stop him. In March 1939 Germany occupied the rest of Czechoslovakia. Hitler then demanded the Polish Corridor from Poland. When the Poles refused, Hitler invaded Poland on 1 September. He was still convinced that Britain and France would not go to war.

Answer 2

The failure of appeasement was certainly one of the main reasons for war. Britain and France wrongly believed that Hitler could be appeased and would be reasonable in his demands. They felt that, if they gave way over the Sudetenland, he would be satisfied and would not want further expansion. The Munich Conference had

Answer 2

exactly the opposite effect. It convinced Hitler that Britain and France would not go to war and encouraged further German expansion in 1939. In March he occupied the rest of Czechoslovakia and in September invaded Poland when they refused to accept his demands for the Polish Corridor.

However, appeasement was not the only or the most important reason. The war was caused mainly by Hitler's aggressive foreign policy. He built up Germany to be a major military power and was not frightened to use that power to get his own way. He remilitarised the Rhineland and occupied Austria. Then he forced the Czechs to give him the Sudetenland. He did not seem to care that he was breaking the Treaty of Versailles.

In conclusion, in many respects the two causes - the failure of appeasement and Hitler's aggressive policies - are interlinked. Appeasement was developed in response to Hitler's demands and only failed because it proved impossible to meet all these demands and because Hitler saw the policy as a sign of weakness rather than a means of satisfying limited demands.

Examiner's Comments: Answer 1

3–4 out of 10

The answer does explain appeasement and, in a narrative framework, shows how it failed to stop Hitler. What it does not do, however, is to consider whether appeasement was the most important reason. It has missed out all the other reasons for war, so cannot score more than 4 marks.

Answer 2

9–10 out of 10

This is a very good answer. It gives two developed reasons for the war, appeasement and Hitler's aggressive policies, but constantly focuses on the question and makes a judgement on which was the more important. So far this is a level 3 answer. The conclusion, however, moves it up to level 4 because it makes clear links between the two major causes.

6

Practice Question

Now try to answer this sort of question yourself.

Was the German occupation of Prague in March 1939 the most important reason for the failure of appeasement?   **(10 marks)**

Remember to:

1 Fully explain the reason given in the question.
2 Develop at least two other reasons. Write a good-length paragraph on each.
3 In your conclusion decide which was the most important reason and explain why.

1.6 Why did the USA and the USSR become rivals in the period 1945 to 1949?

1

Topic Summary

In the period immediately after the Second World War there was a 'Cold War' between the democratic, capitalist countries of the West and the communist countries of Eastern Europe. This was not a military conflict. Instead it was a war of words, where propaganda was used to discredit the other side. However, it also involved an arms race which brought the world to the point of nuclear destruction. The rivalry between the two superpowers emerged at the end of the Second World War especially at the peace conferences of Yalta and Postdam, but grew worse because of the Truman Doctrine, Marshall Plan and the Berlin Crisis.

2

What do I Need to Know?

You will need to know the origins and reasons for the Cold War and the decisions made at Yalta and Potsdam. Examiners will also expect a knowledge of Soviet expansion in Eastern Europe 1945-49, the 'Iron Curtain', the Truman Doctrine and Marshall Plan and events in Berlin 1945-49, especially the Berlin Blockade and airlift.

3

Rivalry between USA and USSR, 1945–49

The early years, 1945–46

- During the Second World War the Soviet Union had fought on the same side as the USA and the other Allies. However, even before the end of the War it became obvious that there were disagreements between the US and Soviet 'sides'.

- At the Yalta Conference in February 1945, attended by Churchill (Britain), Roosevelt (USA) and Stalin (USSR), it was agreed that Germany would be divided into four zones. These would be run by the USA, Britain, France and the Soviet Union. Berlin (which was in the Soviet zone) was also divided into four zones.

- The Potsdam Conference of July–August 1945 was attended by Stalin, Attlee (the new British Prime Minister who replaced

Churchill) and the new US President, Truman (Roosevelt had died in April). There were several areas of tension:

o Stalin wanted to take reparations from Germany but this was opposed by Britain and the USA who did not want to cripple Germany.

o President Truman did not tell Stalin about the atomic bomb before the USA first used it in August 1945.

o Stalin had set up a communist government in Poland despite promising free elections.

Reasons for the Cold War

The reasons for the Cold War can be summed up in one word – distrust. Both the Soviets and the Americans simply did not trust each other. Why was this?

- They had completely different political beliefs. The Soviet Union was communist, with few rights and little freedom for its citizens, and a state-controlled economy with no free enterprise. The USA was a democracy, with elections and greater freedom for its citizens. It also had a capitalist economy.

- Each side was convinced that the other wanted to spread its beliefs at the expense of the other.

- During the early twentieth century the Soviet Union had become convinced that the West was happy to see it attacked. For example, the West had sent help to the Whites during the Russian Civil War of 1918–21.

- The Soviet Union also thought that the dropping of the atomic bomb on Hiroshima was really a warning to them from the USA.

- At the end of the War the Soviet Union set up a communist 'buffer zone' on its western border. The Soviets said this was a defensive barrier. The Americans saw it as the first step towards communist world domination.

- Truman was much more suspicious of the USSR than Roosevelt. He was determined to prevent the spread of communism.

Summary box 1

31

Developments in the Cold War, 1947–48

The Cold War really intensified in this period because of several developments:

- After the Second World War the Soviet Union set up communist 'puppet' governments in Poland, Albania, Bulgaria, Yugoslavia, Czechoslovakia, Romania and Hungary. In a speech at Fulton, Missouri in March 1946 Churchill said an 'Iron Curtain' had fallen across Europe.
- The Soviets said this gave them protection against the West, but the US feared that as one country became communist so would the next, and so on.
- Truman feared the spread of communism into Greece. In 1947 the USA supplied Greece with arms, supplies and money: the communists were defeated. Truman made a speech setting out how his country would support people against communist aggression. This was called the Truman Doctrine.
- Truman believed that poverty and hardship provided a breeding ground for communism and so he wished to make Europe prosperous again. Under the Marshall Plan, set up in June 1947, the Americans gave economic aid to European countries. $13 billion poured into Europe in the years 1947-51. This worsened the Cold War because Stalin accused the Americans of trying to control the trade and economy of Europe. He refused to allow the countries of Eastern Europe to accept this aid.

The Berlin Crisis, 1948–49

- After the Second World War Germany and its capital had been divided into four zones of occupation. In 1948 the French, US and British zones merged to become West Germany. With the help of Marshall Aid, West Germany and West Berlin recovered and began to prosper. It was a different story in East Germany and East Berlin. Here there was poverty and hunger. Many East Germans were leaving the East because West Germany seemed more attractive.
- In Stalin's eyes it seemed that the Allies were building up West Germany in order to attack him. When they introduced a new West German currency, the Deutschmark, this was the last straw. He tried to blockade Berlin. In June 1948 Stalin closed all road and rail connections from Berlin to West Germany hoping he could force the Western Allies out of Berlin.
- Stalin could not block the air corridors to West Berlin without provoking war so the Allies decided to airlift supplies to West Berlin to prevent its people from starving. The airlift was a great success. Every day thousands of British and American planes flew supplies to overcome the Blockade. By May 1949 the USSR lifted the Blockade.

- This was a victory for the West but relations with the USSR hit rock bottom and Germany would now remain divided. The Federal Republic of Germany (West Germany) was decreed in August 1949; in October 1949 the Soviet zone became the German Democratic Republic (East Germany).

4 What do I Know?

Why did the following bring about the Cold War:

- Disagreements over Germany
- Differences in ideology
- Soviet policy in Eastern Europe
- Mutual distrust?

1 Name the two Allied conferences of 1945.
2 Who were the three leaders who attended each of these conferences?
3 What was the 'Iron Curtain'?
4 Why did Stalin want to control the countries of Eastern Europe?
5 What was the Truman Doctrine?
6 What was Marshall Aid?
7 Which European countries did not receive this aid?
8 What happened to Berlin in 1945?
9 Why did Stalin decide to blockade Berlin in 1948?
10 What happened to Germany after the Berlin Crisis of 1948–49?

My score ......

5 Exam Type Question

Here is the sort of source-based question you might be asked in an exam paper. Look closely at the answers given and the examiner's comments on them. Then answer the practice question.

> The crisis was planned in Washington, behind a smokescreen of anti-Soviet propaganda. In 1948 there was danger of war. The conduct of the Western powers risked bloody incidents. The self-blockade of the Western powers hit the West Berlin population with harshness. The people were freezing and starving. In the spring of 1949 the USA was forced to yield. Their war plans had come to nothing, because of the conduct of the USSR.

▲ **An official statement on the Berlin Blockade issued by the Soviet Union after the crisis was over.**

> According to the source, what were the results of the Berlin Crisis of 1948–49? **(3 marks)**

Answer 1

> The Berlin blockade was planned in Berlin and it was the Western powers who almost caused war. As a result of the crisis the USA had to give in.

Answer 2

> According to the source the Berlin Crisis had several results. Firstly it badly affected the people of West Berlin who were 'freezing and starving'. Secondly the writer believes that it was a diplomatic defeat for the USA. Linked to this, the official statement believes that the failure of the USA policy was due to the actions taken by the USSR.

Examiner's Comments: Answer 1

1 out of 3

This is not well focused on the question, with only one consequence identified. The first sentence is not directly relevant because it mentions causation.

Answer 2

3 out of 3

This is a well-focused answer which identifies three results of the Berlin Crisis.

6

Practice Question

Now try to answer this sort of question yourself.

> At Potsdam we were faced with accomplished facts and were forced to agree to a Russian occupation of Eastern Poland. It was a high-handed outrage. Unless Russia is faced with an iron fist and strong language another war is in the making. Only one language do they understand – 'How many divisions have you?' I'm tired of babying the Soviets.

▲ **Extract from a letter sent to US Secretary of State Byrnes by President Truman, January 1946.**

According to the source, why was Truman opposed to the Soviet Union? **(3 marks)**

For this type of question you are awarded a mark for every relevant point you make. Try to explain at least three relevant points from the source.

1.7 How did the Cold War develop in the period 1949 to 1963?

...1

Topic Summary

This period saw the emergence of two rival alliance systems – NATO for the West and the Warsaw Pact for the Soviet Union and Eastern Europe – and the beginning of the nuclear arms race. The Cold War spread to Asia with the outbreak of war in Korea in 1950 but the death of Stalin led to a temporary thaw in East–West relations under his successor, Khrushchev. This was short-lived with further problems in Hungary in 1956, the U2 Crisis in 1960, the construction of the Berlin Wall in 1961 and the Cuban Missile Crisis in 1962.

...2

What do I Need to Know?

You will need to answer questions on the key developments in this period especially the causes, events and results of the Korean War and Hungarian Rising and the features of Khruschev's policy of co-existence. You will also need to know the significance of the U2 Crisis of 1960 and the building of the Berlin Wall and the causes, events and results of the Cuban Missile Crisis of 1962.

...3

Development of the Cold War, 1949–63

The Korean War, 1950–53

- At the end of the Second World War, Korea was split into two along the 38th parallel: the USSR took control of North Korea and set up a communist state. In the South, the Americans set up a democracy. The South Korean President (Syngman Rhee) and the North Korean President (Kim Il Sung) each claimed to be President of Korea. Relations were tense. In June 1950 North Korea invaded South Korea.
- At first the South Korean forces were pushed back. President Truman asked the United Nations Organisation to help. UN forces from many countries, but mainly the USA, drove the communists back until they were close to the Yalu River on the border with China.
- This worried China, which did not want a non-communist neighbour supported by US troops. China joined the war. The UN forces were driven back and the UN commander, General MacArthur, called for the use of nuclear weapons. Truman rejected MacArthur's aggressive stance and sacked him.

- Once again UN troops began to push the communists back. By June 1951 the fighting had settled around the 38th parallel. In 1953 Stalin died, which made the communists want to end the war as quickly as possible. A truce was agreed at Panmunjom.

- Although the USA had stopped communist expansion to the South, Korea remained divided into two states.

Fluctuating relations, 1949–56

- By 1955 there were two rival alliances. In 1949 Western Europe, Canada and the USA set up the North Atlantic Treaty Organisation (NATO). Its main purpose was to defend each of its members. If one member was attacked, all the others would help to defend this member. In 1955 West Germany joined NATO. The Soviet response was to set up the Warsaw Pact – a communist version of NATO.

- As relations between the USA and the Soviet Union worsened, both sides began to develop their weapons so as to be able to 'outgun' their opponents. By 1949 both the USA and the Soviet Union had nuclear weapons. Then in 1952 the Americans developed the hydrogen bomb (H-bomb) which was capable of destroying Moscow. Within a year the Soviet Union had developed a similar bomb. In 1957 the Soviet Union devised a means of attaching nuclear warheads to rockets.

- Stalin died in 1953 and was eventually replaced by Nikita Khrushchev. He was a less aggressive leader than Stalin and talked of peaceful coexistence (living in peace) with the West. In 1956, at the Twentieth Congress of the Communist Party, he made a secret speech attacking Stalin for being a dictator. Khrushchev also began the process of 'destalinisation'.

- The West began to see hopeful signs from the new Soviet leader which led to a 'thaw' in relations. Khrushchev seemed to be encouraging greater freedom within the USSR and its allies. On a visit to Warsaw in 1956 he indicated that Polish people should be allowed more freedom. This was short-lived due to Soviet reaction to events in Hungary.

The Hungarian Rising, 1956

- In July 1956 a reforming government led by Imre Nagy took power in Hungary after repeated rioting by students in Budapest. The new government planned to increase personal and political freedom and even talked of taking Hungary out of the Warsaw Pact.

- The Soviet response to the reforms was harsh. On 4 November Khrushchev sent 6000 tanks into Hungary to overthrow the rebellion and crush any further protest. The Soviets arrested Nagy and installed a loyalist communist, Kadar, to set up a new government. Nagy was later shot for his part in the rebellion. Soviet troops remained in Budapest until the crisis was over.

- An estimated 30,000 Hungarians were killed during the crisis and 200,000 fled to the West. The Western powers protested about the Soviet interference but did little else.

Crises of 1960–61

The U2 crisis

- On 1 May 1960 the Soviets shot down a US spy plane over the USSR and captured the pilot, Gary Powers. According to the Soviets he admitted he was on a spying mission.
- The US denied that spying flights took place over Soviet territory and claimed that the plane had accidentally strayed into Soviet territory. The Soviets showed that the US were lying by developing the film taken by Powers on his mission. Eisenhower, the President of the USA, refused to apologise.
- This was a diplomatic defeat for the USA. It had lost a U2 spy plane and the Soviets had scored a propaganda victory.

The Berlin Wall

- In August 1961 Khrushchev decided to build a wall around West Berlin. This was to prevent more East Germans moving to the West. Between 1945 and 1960, an estimated 3 million people had crossed from East to West Berlin, many of whom were skilled workers.
- The wall had immediate effects: the flow of refugees stopped instantly. Few people tried to escape, but many of those who did were killed in the attempt: 86 people are known to have died attempting to cross the Berlin Wall between 1961 and 1989. The British and US claimed that having to build the Wall was proof of the poor lifestyle in Eastern Europe.
- John F Kennedy visited West Berlin in 1963 and declared that the city was a symbol of the struggle between the forces of freedom and the communist world.

How close to war did the world come over Cuba in 1962?

- The island of Cuba had once been under US control, but in 1959 Fidel Castro had seized power and set up a pro-communist government. The US disliked having a communist regime so close because they feared that communism would spread to Central and South American countries. In addition, Castro developed very good relations with the USSR.
- The new President of the USA, John F Kennedy, approved an invasion of Cuba in April 1961 designed to overthrow Castro and restore the previous leader, Batista. This 'Bay of Pigs' operation was a disastrous failure and worsened relations between Cuba and the USA.

- Cuba now allowed the Soviet Union to station nuclear weapons on Cuba, within firing range of the USA.

The Crisis

- In October 1962 US planes identified nuclear missile sites being built on Cuba.
- After much debate President Kennedy decided on a naval blockade around Cuba to stop Soviet ships landing nuclear weapons on the island. President Kennedy also threatened to invade Cuba and remove the missiles by force.
- The next ten days were very tense. If the Soviet ships had ignored the blockade and sailed to Cuba, there would have been war between the two countries.
- It was the Soviet leader, Khrushchev, who broke the deadlock. On 24 October he ordered his ships to turn back, and on 28 October he agreed to remove the missiles and return them to the Soviet Union.

Results of the Crisis

The Cuban Missile Crisis had a major effect on East–West relations:

- Leaders of both the USSR and the USA realised that nuclear war had been a real possibility and that it was vital that such a crisis should not happen again.
- The US and USSR decided to set up a telephone link (hot line) so that in future, communications could take place immediately between Moscow and Washington during a crisis.
- Nuclear arms limitation talks began and, in 1963, a Test Ban Treaty was signed between the USA, the USSR and Britain.

Summary box

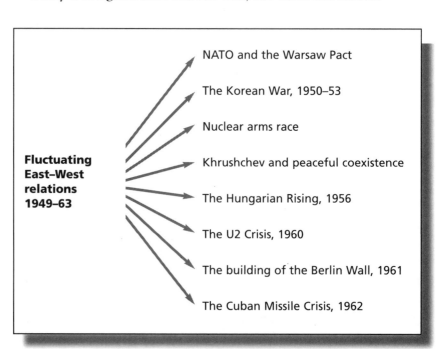

Fluctuating East–West relations 1949–63

- NATO and the Warsaw Pact
- The Korean War, 1950–53
- Nuclear arms race
- Khrushchev and peaceful coexistence
- The Hungarian Rising, 1956
- The U2 Crisis, 1960
- The building of the Berlin Wall, 1961
- The Cuban Missile Crisis, 1962

4
What do I Know?

Why did the following increase tension between the USA and the USSR:

- The Hungarian Rising, 1956
- The U2 spy plane, 1960
- The building of the Berlin Wall, 1961
- The Cuban Missile Crisis, 1962?

1 What does NATO stand for?
2 Why did the USA become involved in the conflict in Korea?
3 Why was General MacArthur dismissed?
4 What organisation was set up by the Soviet Union as a response to NATO?
5 What was peaceful coexistence?
6 Why did the Soviet Union intervene in Hungary in 1956?
7 Who was the pilot of the U2 plane shot down in 1960?
8 In what year was the Berlin Wall built?
9 Who became Cuban leader in 1959?
10 Where was the unsuccessful Cuban invasion of 1961?

My score ......

5
Exam Type Question

Here is the sort of source-based question you might be asked in an exam paper. Look closely at the answers given and the examiner's comments on them. Then answer the practice question.

> I had time to think aboard the plane. In my generation, this was not the first occasion when the strong had attacked the weak. I remembered how each time that the democracies failed to act it had encouraged the aggressors to keep going ahead. Communism was acting in Korea just as Hitler, Mussolini and the Japanese had acted ten, fifteen and twenty years earlier. I felt certain that if South Korea was allowed to fall, Communist leaders would be encouraged to invade nations closer to our shores.

▲ From US President Truman's *Memoirs* on the US involvement in Korea.

How reliable is the source to an historian studying the Korean War? Use the source and your own knowledge to explain your answer.   **(6 marks)**

Answer 1

This is reliable because it is written by Truman who was there. It is also reliable because it tells us that the Communist attack on South Korea was the same as the attacks by Hitler, Mussolini and Japan.

Answer 2

> The source provides a reliable view of Truman's motives for involvement in the Korean War. He certainly did fear the spread of Communism and the 'domino effect' and was determined to avoid the weakness shown against German, Italian and Japanese aggression in the 1930s. His Memoirs gave him the opportunity to reflect on US motives in 1950.
>
> However it is only one very biased view of the Korean War. Truman is trying to justify his own actions in 1950 as well as American involvement in the Korean War and therefore possibly exaggerates the Communist threat, comparing it to the expansion of Hitler and Mussolini.

Examiner's Comments: Answer 1

2 out of 6

This is too brief and takes the contents at face value. There is simplistic evaluation in the first sentence. This would be awarded a lower level 2 and given 2 marks.

Answer 2

6 out of 6

A very good answer which gives a balanced evaluation of the source by discussing the reliability of both its contents and its origin. The student uses his/her own knowledge to assess the purpose and bias of the source.

6

Practice Question

Now try to answer this sort of question yourself.

> The Fascist rebellion in Hungary has been crushed thanks to the resolute action of the Hungarian people and Soviet armed forces fighting the counter-revolution at the Hungarian Government's request.

▲ **A Soviet delegate at the UN General Assembly on Monday, 3 December 1956.**

How reliable is the source to an historian studying the Hungarian Rising of 1956? Use the source and your own knowledge to explain your answer. **(6 marks)**

Remember to look back at page 10 for help with answering questions on reliability.

1.8 The Cold War, 1963–79

1

Topic Summary

In the period 1949–56 there was great fluctuation in relations between the USA and the USSR. The Cuban Missile Crisis brought some improvement but this was short-lived due to the Soviet invasion of Czechoslovakia in 1968. Nevertheless there were genuine attempts at détente in the 1970s because both superpowers sought to reduce the scale of their nuclear arms programmes. This ended in 1979 with the Soviet invasion of Afghanistan.

2

What do I Need to Know?

You will need to have a thorough knowledge of the Czechoslovakian Crisis of 1968, the consequences of the Vietnam War, reasons for détente and the arms limitations talks in the 1970s. You will also need to know what was achieved by détente, and how successful it was in improving relations between East and West and reducing the arms race.

3

The Cold War, 1963–79

Czechoslovakia, 1968

- In January 1968 Dubcek was elected as leader of the Communist Party in Czechoslovakia. He promised a number of reforms, including the freedom to travel abroad, the end of press censorship and less state control. He promised 'socialism with a human face'. His reforms became known as the 'Prague Spring'.
- The Soviet leader, Brezhnev, was alarmed by the reforms – to allow them would weaken communism – and in August sent troops into Czechoslovakia to remove Dubcek. His reforms were stopped and censorship reintroduced. In 1969 Dubcek resigned and was replaced by a loyal communist, Husak.
- As with Hungary in 1956, the Western powers did little to assist those in conflict with the Soviet leadership. Both China and the West condemned Soviet action, but did nothing to help Dubcek and his government.
- The Soviets justified the invasion as conforming to the Brezhnev Doctrine – the right to prevent any member leaving the Warsaw Pact.

The effects of the war in Vietnam

By 1973 the USA had withdrawn most of its troops from the conflict in Vietnam. This had several effects on the Cold War:

- The withdrawal of US forces was seen as a defeat and was a blow to the morale of the American people. The USA became far less willing to get involved in foreign conflicts.

- By 1975 both Laos and Cambodia had communist governments. Instead of slowing it down, US policies had actually speeded up the domino effect in the region.
- The USA were now determined to improve relations with communist countries. Containment gave way to co-operation. This, in turn, encouraged greater links with China and a period of greater understanding with the USSR.

Détente

By the end of the 1960s there was a general relaxation in tension between the superpowers. This easing of tension became known as détente.

Reasons for détente

Détente developed for several reasons:

- The Vietnam War had damaged the confidence of the USA. Americans were keen to find ways to avoid further conflict.
- The cost of the nuclear arms race was escalating. The arms race was based on the policy of Mutually Assured Destruction (MAD). This meant that, in theory, neither side would use nuclear weapons because the other side would retaliate – and both sides would be destroyed. Both the USA and the Soviet Union had economic problems during the 1970s.
- In the USA there was rising inflation. This, together with spending on the Vietnam War, was crippling the US economy. The Americans wanted to reduce expenditure on arms in order to increase spending on poverty at home.
- The Soviet Union had low living standards and poor industrial efficiency, and needed to trade more with the West.
- Both superpowers were worried about the conflict in the Middle East. Oil supplies from that area were vital for both countries, and the Suez Canal was important for sea routes. Communist and non-communist countries had become involved in the conflict there between Arabs and Israelis.
- The hostility between China and the USSR meant that there was no longer the simple situation of a single communist country facing the capitalist countries of the West.
- For the USA détente was a way of further dividing the USSR from China.
- For the Chinese détente was an opportunity to develop relations with the USA and end its isolation.

Key features of détente

- In 1969 the USA and USSR began the Strategic Arms Limitation Talks (SALT) in an effort to control the arms race. The talks lasted for three years and in 1972 SALT 1 was signed.
- In 1975 the Helsinki Agreement was made. It recognised the borders of Eastern Europe and Soviet influence in that area. In addition, all countries agreed to improve human rights.

- In 1979 the USA and Soviet Union agreed to further reductions of arms at talks in Vienna known as SALT 2.
- The superpowers even began to co-operate in space. In July 1975 three US astronauts and two Soviet cosmonauts docked their Apollo and Soyuz spacecraft together in orbit around the earth.
- Relations improved between the USA and China. Visits by US and Chinese table tennis teams to each other's countries in 1971–72 led to the term 'ping pong diplomacy'. In 1972 US President Nixon made an historic visit to Peking. Trade talks and improved relations followed.

Summary box

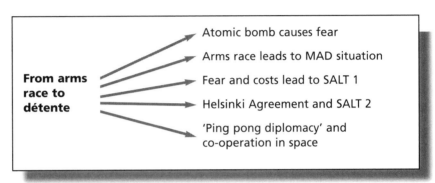

From arms race to détente
- Atomic bomb causes fear
- Arms race leads to MAD situation
- Fear and costs lead to SALT 1
- Helsinki Agreement and SALT 2
- 'Ping pong diplomacy' and co-operation in space

4

What do I Know?

1 Who became leader of Czechoslovakia in the spring of 1968?
2 What were his reforms known as?
3 Who replaced him as leader?
4 What was the Brezhnev Doctrine?
5 What does MAD stand for?
6 What does SALT stand for?
7 Who was the US President who visited China?
8 What was 'ping pong diplomacy'?
9 Name the agreement made in 1975.
10 When was the SALT 2 agreement made?

My score ......

Why did both the USA and USSR favour détente in the 1970s?

5

Exam Type Question

Here is the sort of question you might be asked in an exam paper. Look closely at the answer given and the examiner's comments on it. Then answer the practice question.

Describe how the Soviet Union crushed reform in Czechoslovakia in 1968.   **(6 marks)**

Answer

> In 1968 Dubcek, the new leader of the Communist Party in Czechoslovakia, introduced reforms including a relaxation of censorship. The Soviet Union sent in troops and arrested Dubcek. This was because of the Brezhnev Doctrine.

Examiner's Comments

3 out of 6

This answer is too brief. This is a pity because it has the main points but does not explain them. For example there is no explanation of the Brezhnev Doctrine. To get full marks the answer would need to describe in greater detail the significance of the three events mentioned. I think this answer would score, at best, half marks.

6

Practice Question

Now try to answer this sort of question yourself.

Describe how relations between the superpowers improved in the 1970s. **(6 marks)**

Remember that to answer this question:

1 You need to give a detailed description of the factor or factors mentioned in the question. If there are two factors, explain each in detail.
2 Be precise in your description.
3 Write two good-length paragraphs because this question is worth 6 marks.

1.9 The last years of the Cold War, 1979–91

1 Topic Summary

Détente ended with the Soviet invasion of Afghanistan in 1979. It was followed by a period of superpower rivalry with the USA boycotting the Moscow Olympics of 1980 and the re-emergence of the nuclear arms race. The Solidarity movement emerged and threatened communist control of Poland. Gorbachev became Soviet leader in 1985 and began a series of reforms which not only changed the USSR but hastened the overthrow of communist control of Eastern Europe and the end of the Cold War.

2 What do I Need to Know?

You are expected to know about the Soviet invasion of Afghanistan and its effects on Soviet–US relations, the renewal of the Cold War under Reagan, including Star Wars, the impact of the Solidarity movement in Poland, Gorbachev's reforms in the USSR and their impact on Eastern Europe, and the collapse of Soviet control in Eastern Europe and its implications.

3 The last years of the Cold War, 1979–91

Afghanistan, 1979

In 1979 the Soviet Union invaded Afghanistan. This was for several reasons:

- The Soviets were concerned about the Muslim revolution in neighbouring Iran which could have spread to Afghanistan and Muslim areas inside the Soviet Union.
- The political situation in Afghanistan was very unstable at the end of the 1970s and the Soviets wanted to maintain their influence in the area.
- Afghanistan is close to the Middle East oil reserves of the Western powers and the ports of the Indian Ocean. The Soviets were interested in developing their interests in this area.

Within weeks of the invasion Soviet troops were being attacked by the Mujaheddin (Afghan Islamic fighters) using guerrilla tactics. The invasion of Afghanistan brought a return to Cold War tensions:

- The US refused to ratify SALT 2.
- They boycotted the Moscow Olympics in 1980.
- They stopped grain shipments to the Soviet Union and they increased aid to the Afghan rebels.
- The Soviet Union faced hostility from other Muslim nations such as Pakistan. This worried the Soviets who feared opposition from some of the Muslim communities within the USSR.

US–Soviet relations in the 1980s

Superpower relations in the 1980s were dominated by US President Reagan and Mikhail Gorbachev of the USSR.

- Reagan was elected US President in 1980. He did not trust the USSR. He began to build up US defence forces and spending, and ordered further research into the Strategic Defence Initiative (SDI) or 'Star Wars' programme, a satellite anti-missile system.

- In the USSR, Brezhnev had continued to support hard-line communist policies up until his death in 1982. Three years later Gorbachev became leader of the Soviet Union and immediately set about improving relations with the USA. He realised that the USSR could not afford to continue an arms race with the USA. After several meetings, the USSR and USA signed an Intermediate Nuclear Forces (INF) Treaty which removed all medium-range nuclear weapons from Europe.

- The war in Afghanistan could not be won. Following a meeting between Reagan and Gorbachev in 1988, an agreement was reached. The last Soviet troops left Afghanistan in February 1989.

- SALT had developed into START (Strategic Arms Reduction Talks) and Gorbachev also proposed big cuts in non-nuclear US and Soviet forces.

Solidarity in Poland

- By the late 1970s there was considerable unrest in Poland. Many Poles did not support the communist government because of economic problems, low pay, lack of freedom and opposition to the strong Roman Catholic Church.

- In 1980 a series of strikes in the shipyards in the Polish port of Gdansk (formerly Danzig) led to the formation of a new independent trade union called Solidarity.

- Solidarity, led by shipyard worker Lech Walesa, caught the imagination of the Polish people and had the support of the Catholic Church. Strikes spread to many other industries.

- At first the Polish government made concessions, including the right to form trade unions. When these failed to stem the growth of Solidarity, the Polish Communist Party called for sterner measures to deal with the crisis and brought in a tougher leader called General Jaruzelski.

- In 1981 the more extreme members of Solidarity demanded reforms which called into being the very existence of the Communist Party in Poland. Brezhnev issued an ultimatum: sort out the situation at once or face the possibility of invasion and having Poland's essential raw materials (including oil) cut off.

- Jaruzelski banned Solidarity, ordered the arrest and detention of Lech Walesa and other leaders, and declared a national state of emergency. The secret police arrested nearly 7000 political opponents and killed a number of people. Solidarity went underground.

- The emergence of Gorbachev as Soviet leader changed the situation in Poland. After Gorbachev's visit to Warsaw in 1988, Jaruzelski began talks with Solidarity which ended in agreement to lift the ban on the union, allow opposition parties to be formed and to go ahead with free elections. In 1989 Poland elected their first non-communist leader. A year later Lech Walesa was elected President of Poland by a huge majority.

- Solidarity was important because it was the first serious attack on communist control on Eastern Europe in the 1980s and inspired opposition in other Eastern European countries.

The collapse of the Soviet Empire

Gorbachev's policies
When Gorbachev came to power he introduced two policies in the USSR:

- *Glasnost* (openness). Gorbachev wanted to end the intense secrecy which surrounded what happened in the Soviet Union.

- *Perestroika* (restructuring). Gorbachev believed that the time had come to open up Soviet politics, to allow promotion on the grounds of efficiency (instead of Communist Party loyalty) and to allow market forces in the Soviet economy.

End of communist domination in Eastern Europe
Part of Gorbachev's new openness involved explaining his policies to the people and trying to win their support. This new attitude also involved changes in Soviet control of Eastern Europe. In 1989 he informed the other communist powers in this area that they could no longer expect support from the Red Army.

By 1989 it was clear that Gorbachev's policies inside the Soviet Union were not working. The economy was in ruins and the leaders did not seem to know what to do. The people of Eastern Europe saw their chance for political freedom and in a series of spontaneous uprisings overthrew their communist rulers.

As communist governments fell across Europe it was apparent that the Cold War was over – an event best symbolised by the dismantling of the Berlin Wall in 1989. In 1991 the Warsaw Pact was formally ended.

Summary box 1

End of communism in Eastern Europe, 1989		
Month	**Country**	**Event**
March	Hungary	Border with non-communist Austria dismantled
June	Poland	Non-communist leader (Walesa) elected
September	East Germany	Thousands of citizens escape to Austria and West Germany
October	East Germany	Troops refuse to fire on demonstrators
November	East Germany	Berlin Wall pulled down
November	Czechoslovakia	Opening of borders with West
December	Romania	Communist leader, Ceausescu, overthrown
December	Hungary	Free elections announced
December	Bulgaria	Mass demonstrations against communist government

End of the Soviet Union

- The Soviet Union itself lasted only a little longer. Soon republics began demanding their freedom from Soviet control.
- Gorbachev found it increasingly difficult to maintain control, especially in 1991 when there was an attempted coup against him and it became clear that Boris Yeltsin was the man with the power in the Soviet Union. Finally, the Soviet Union was replaced by the Commonwealth of Independent States (CIS). Russia, led by Boris Yeltsin, was now a partner, not ruler, of the other republics.

Summary box 2

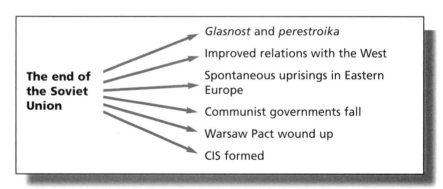

Implications for world affairs

The break-up of the Soviet Union and the end of its control over Eastern Europe had immediate effects:

- The Cold War ended and the arms race was over.
- This did not mean the end of troubles in Eastern Europe. In January 1993 Czechoslovakia split into two separate states, the Czech Republic and Slovakia.

- The worst troubles were in the former Yugoslavia as a number of areas tried to win independence after the collapse of communist control. The Serbs refused to accept a Croat as leader, and both Serbia and Croatia declared independence in 1991. The resulting civil war led to the so-called 'ethnic cleansing'.
- East and West Berlin were reunited in 1991, and East and West Germany became a single country.

4

What do I Know?

What part did the following play in ending communist control of Eastern Europe:
- The Solidarity movement
- Gorbachev's policies in the Soviet Union
- Gorbachev's declaration of 1989?

1　What does SDI stand for?

2　What replaced SALT?

3　Who became leader of the USSR in 1985?

4　What is meant by *glasnost*?

5　What name was given to the policy of reconstruction in the Soviet Union?

6　Who led the Solidarity movement in Poland?

7　In what year was the Berlin Wall pulled down?

8　What does CIS stand for?

9　What happened to Gorbachev in 1991?

My score ......

5

Exam Type Question

Here is the sort of causation question you might be asked in an exam paper. Look closely at the answer given and the examiner's comments on it. Then answer the practice question.

Was the Solidarity movement the most important reason for the end of Soviet control of Eastern Europe?　**(10 marks)**

Answer

Solidarity was set up in Poland in 1980 and organised strikes and asked for reforms such as more freedom. The leader was a shipyard worker called Lech Walesa. At first Solidarity got reforms but then the Soviet Union forced the Polish government to ban Solidarity and arrest its leaders. Eventually, in 1988, the ban was lifted and the following year Lech Walesa became the President of Poland.

> Gorbachev became Soviet leader in 1985 and introduced new policies such as *glasnost*, which means openness, and *perestroika* which means reconstruction. The USSR now had a market economy and greater freedom. In 1989 Gorbachev made it clear that the Red Army would no longer support the communist powers in Eastern Europe.
>
> In most of the Iron Curtain countries the people had turned against communism because they wanted prosperity and greater freedom. In November 1989 the people of East Germany pulled down the Berlin Wall.

Examiner's Comments

4 out of 10

This is a narrative approach to the question which implies causation but fails to focus on the question. It has the main reasons for the collapse of Soviet control – Solidarity, Gorbachev and the attitude of the peoples of the Eastern European countries. It does not address the key issue of whether Solidarity was the most important reason nor does it assess the importance of the other reasons.

6

Practice Question

Now try to answer this sort of question yourself.

Why were there improved relations between the USA and USSR in the years after 1985? **(10 marks)**

Remember that to answer this question:

- You need to fully develop at least two reasons. Write a good-length paragraph on each.
- Either link the reasons or decide, with a detailed explanation, which is the most important.

2 Britain in the First World War

2.1 What part was played by Britain in the defeat of Germany on the Western Front?

Topic Summary

When war broke out in 1914 most people expected a quick war, but it was to last for four years and result in the death of millions of young men. Much of the fighting took place on the French and Belgium border in an area known as the Western Front. The British played an important part in the defeat of the Germans in this area. In 1914 they helped to defeat the Schlieffen Plan. For the next three years the British launched several important attacks, and developed new weapons and methods of fighting, such as tanks and the creeping barrage. The British also played a leading role in the attacks of 1918 which forced Germany to agree to an armistice.

What do I Need to Know?

You will be expected to know the part played by the British in preventing a German breakthrough and victory in 1914, and how the system of trenches developed. You will need to know the nature of trench warfare, both in terms of military strategy and its effects on the soldiers involved. You will also need to assess the role of new weapons in the fighting, and the significance of the Battle of the Somme. Finally, you will need to know about the events of 1918, especially Ludendorff's Spring Offensives and the Allied drive to victory.

Britain and the defeat of Germany on the Western Front

The BEF and the events of 1914

On 3 August 1914 the Germans launched the Schlieffen Plan and invaded Belgium. The Plan relied on speed, but by mid-September it had failed. This was partly due to the role of the British Expeditionary Force (BEF), but there were other factors:

- The Belgians held up the German advance using their forts at Antwerp, Liege and Namur.

- This delay enabled the BEF to play a part. The BEF started arriving in France as early as 15 August and held up the German advance at Mons (20 August) and Le Cateau (26 August).
- This, in turn, gave the French the time to turn northwards to face the German advance.
- The Russians were able to mobilise their troops in just ten days, not the six weeks as expected.
- The German advance was eventually halted by the French and BEF forces at the Battle of the Marne in early September with the Germans forced to retreat northwards to the River Aisne.
- As the Germans retreated to areas that were easier to defend, they set up a series of trenches that stretched from the English Channel to the Swiss border. The British and French in turn set up trenches to protect their men.
- The failure of the Schlieffen Plan meant that there was no quick end to the war and the Germans would now have to fight a war on two fronts.
- In October the Germans tried to capture the Channel ports in order to cut off British supplies and reinforcements. This attempt failed when the BEF held the German advance at the First Battle of Ypres, October–November 1914. This meant that the channel ports were in Allied hands, so Britain could continue to transport troops and supplies to France.

Summary box 1

Reasons why the war went on
- Failure of Schlieffen Plan
- Belgian defences
- Early arrival of BEF
- Russian mobilisation
- Establishment of trenches

Trench warfare

The trench system became stronger and more sophisticated as the war progressed. The area in between the two sides' trenches was known as No Man's Land, with all trees, vegetation and buildings destroyed by constant bombardment. It became a wilderness, with shell holes filled with water in which many soldiers drowned. The men lived in the trenches and slept in dug-outs which were little better than holes in the sides of the trenches. Soldiers spent about ten to fourteen days at a time in the front line and they could not rest or sleep properly due to regular shelling. Conditions were very unpleasant:

- The British trenches were in Flanders where it frequently rained, causing flooding. Some men suffered from 'trench foot', the water causing their feet to swell and rot.

- Food was not pleasant, often having to be eaten cold with dried, hard biscuits.
- The trenches were very unhygienic and there were lice and rats, the latter attracted by rotting bodies left in No Man's Land.
- Boredom was the major problem because most of the time the men did not fight and, apart from routine duties, they had little to occupy their time.
- There were many dangers, such as being gassed, shot by a sniper, injured by artillery fire or being sent 'over the top'.
- Some soldiers suffered psychological damage due to the horrors of trench warfare and seeing friends being killed. This was known as 'shell-shock'.
- Most soldiers, enthusiastic when they joined the army, became disillusioned once they had experienced trench warfare. Some even shot themselves so they could be sent home to 'blighty'.

The stalemate

Neither side was able to achieve a successful breakthrough on the Western Front between the end of 1914 and 1918. This was for several reasons:

- The trenches were well defended and very difficult to capture. Attackers would have to climb out of their trenches and advance towards the enemy across No Man's Land. They would have to overcome many obstacles such as barbed wire, shell holes, mud and water, even dead bodies. As they advanced across No Man's Land, they were often easy targets for the enemy's machine-gun fire. Even when an enemy trench was captured, there were often not enough men to hold it.
- The commanders on both sides stuck to traditional military tactics in dealing with trench warfare. Haig, the British commander, believed in attrition (wearing the enemy down until they surrendered). This meant frequent attacks, sending wave after wave of men across No Man's Land, resulting in heavy casualties.
- Neither side made full or correct use of the new weapons that were developed, while some, such as gas, were not effective enough to break the stalemate.

Summary box 2

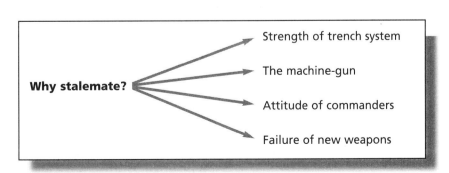

Why stalemate?
- Strength of trench system
- The machine-gun
- Attitude of commanders
- Failure of new weapons

New weapons

New weapons were needed to break the deadlock:

- In April 1915, at Ypres, the Germans first used gas as a weapon. However, gas-masks were soon developed to protect soldiers. There was also the danger of the wind changing direction and gas blowing back on to your own men.

- Artillery was used throughout the war. Both sides used huge field-guns to bombard the enemy trenches, especially before an attack. But this was not effective: it warned the enemy that there was to be an attack and churned up No Man's Land, creating even more hazardous shell holes. There was often a gap of several minutes when the bombardment stopped before the men went over the top. This was enough time for the enemy soldiers to return to their machine-gun posts.

- The British developed the creeping barrage which was first used at the Somme in September 1916. This was a combined artillery bombardment and infantry attack which meant the enemy had to remain in the trenches.

- Tanks came into use in 1916. Sometimes they were very successful but they were slow, clumsy and easily got stuck in the mud, and they often broke down. The use of tanks did not have a major impact until 1918.

- Aeroplanes were used to spy on enemy positions, but the technology had not been developed for planes to attack and bomb these positions.

The Somme, 1916

Each side made many attempts to break through to the enemy's trenches in the period 1915–17. Most of these offensives were by the Allies because the Germans were content to defend the territory they had captured in France and Belgium. The most famous offensive took place on the Somme between July and November 1916. This attack was launched for a variety of reasons:

- The French had been attacked by the Germans at Verdun in February 1916. They were being hard-pressed and wanted a British attack to ease the pressure.

- Haig believed in a policy of attrition and wanted to wear down the Germans through constant attacks.

- The Somme was chosen because it was the area which linked the French and British armies, and this was to be a joint offensive.

Battle of the Somme: a disaster?

- The preliminary bombardment did not destroy the German trenches or barbed wire as had been planned.

- There was no secrecy: the Germans knew well in advance that there was to be an attack and had strengthened their defences.
- In any case the Somme was the strongest part of the German trenches, with dug-outs 10 metres below ground level. The defenders retreated to these dug-outs during the bombardment and then quickly returned to their machine-gun positions once it ended.
- The French forces could not give much help because they were preoccupied with defending Verdun.
- On the first day, 1 July, nearly 60,000 British troops were killed or wounded. There was no breakthrough.
- Haig continued the offensives for a further three months with no breakthrough and incurred casualties of over 400,000.
- Tanks were used for the first time in September but most broke down.

Battle of the Somme: not a total failure

- In August the Germans called off their attack on Verdun.
- The creeping barrage was used successfully to capture two villages.
- The Germans had suffered heavy casualties of over 250,000. They were now exhausted and remained on the defensive throughout 1917.

Summary box 3

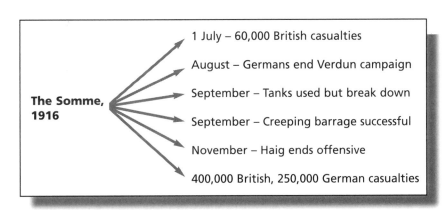

The Somme, 1916

- 1 July – 60,000 British casualties
- August – Germans end Verdun campaign
- September – Tanks used but break down
- September – Creeping barrage successful
- November – Haig ends offensive
- 400,000 British, 250,000 German casualties

3

Defeat of Germany

The defeat of Germany in 1918

In March 1918 the Germans gambled on all-out victory by attacking on the Western Front. They launched the Spring Offensives for several reasons:

- The withdrawal of Russia from the war at the end of 1917. Germany was able to transfer 1 million troops to the Western Front.

- The entry of the USA into the war in April 1917. It would take the USA over a year to recruit, train and send troops to the Western Front. Germany needed to win the war before the Americans could make a decisive contribution.
- The British blockade of Germany was slowly starving the German civilian population.

Ludendorff's Spring Offensives

Ludendorff concentrated his attacks on the British, believing they were exhausted after their offensives of 1917 and convinced that, if they were defeated, the French would soon collapse. Using new tactics the Germans achieved immediate success and drove back the British 50 kilometres in certain places. The main attacks were Operation Michael (March 1918), Operation Georgette (April) and Operation Blücher (May). However, there was no breakthrough.

Allied success

Between July and November 1918 the Allies launched a series of counter-attacks which forced the Germans to retreat. The Allies recovered the land gained during the German Spring Offensives and advanced through Belgium and France and towards the border with Germany. On 11 November 1918 the Germans agreed to an armistice (ceasefire). The German defeat was due to several reasons:

- Ludendorff's gamble had failed. By June 1918 there was no breakthrough and the German troops were exhausted. They had sustained heavier losses than the Allies and had a much greater area to defend.
- The US troops began to arrive in numbers. They provided a morale booster for the Allies and gave them a distinct numerical superiority.
- Germany's allies, including Austria, Turkey and Bulgaria, were defeated.
- The British blockade left the German civilian population seriously short of food and the army deficient in supplies and weaponry. The morale in Germany was at an all-time 'low' because of defeats on the Western Front, serious food shortages and a flu epidemic which killed many undernourished civilians.
- The Allies made effective use of tanks and the creeping barrage in their counter-attacks. Tanks, especially, helped to break through the German defences.
- On 9 November Kaiser Wilhelm abdicated and was replaced by a republican government which was advised by the military leaders to agree to an armistice.

Summary box 4

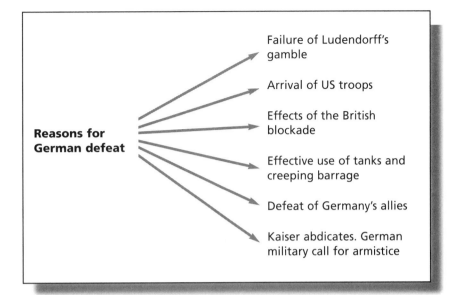

Reasons for German defeat

- Failure of Ludendorff's gamble
- Arrival of US troops
- Effects of the British blockade
- Effective use of tanks and creeping barrage
- Defeat of Germany's allies
- Kaiser abdicates. German military call for armistice

4

What do I Know?

What was important about:

- The failure of the Schlieffen Plan
- Stalemate on the Western Front
- The Battle of the Somme?

1 Which German plan failed and created the need for trenches?

2 At which battle in September 1914 was the German advance finally stopped?

3 What was the significance of the First Battle of Ypres, October 1914?

4 What was the area between the two sets of trenches called?

5 What was the name given to the rotting of feet caused by water in the trenches?

6 Which new weapon could affect your troops as well as the enemy's?

7 When and where were tanks first used on the Western Front?

8 What was the creeping barrage?

9 Give one reason why Ludendorff launched his Spring Offensives of 1918.

My score ......

5

Exam Type Question

Here is the sort of source-based question you might be asked in an exam paper. Look closely at the answers given and the examiner's comments on them. Then answer the practice question.

Source A

▼ **Painting showing Canadian troops being attacked by the Germans in 1915.**

What does Source A tell us about the fighting on the Western Front?   **(3 marks)**

Answer

The painting tells us a lot about the fighting on the Western Front. It shows the strong defences backed up by the machine guns and barbed wire. It also shows how difficult it was for the attackers, who have no cover in No Man's Land and are easy targets for the machine-gunners. Finally it reveals the casualties during attacks on the Western Front. There are Canadian dead and wounded in the trenches and German casualties in No Man's Land.

Examiner's Comments

3 out of 3

An excellent answer. It has managed to make at least three significant interpretations of fighting in the trenches from this source.

6

Practice Question

Source B

Now try to answer this sort of question yourself.

▲ A tank abandoned in No Man's Land.

What does Source B tell us about conditions on the Western Front?
(3 marks)

Remember that for this type of question:

1 You need to pick out three factors because you will be given a mark for each relevant point.

2 Do not write too much. This is worth only 3 marks.

2.2 How important was the role of Britain in the war at sea?

1

Topic Summary

The British navy played a key role in the defeat of Germany. The navy was vital to Britain to prevent a German invasion, protect British trade and communications with the Empire and the Western Front, and also as a means of blockading Germany. Germany threatened Britain in several ways: the German fleet raided the British east coast and tried to attack the British fishing fleet at Dogger Bank; German submarines, known as U-boats, tried to starve Britain out of the war.

2

What do I Need to Know?

You will be expected to have knowledge and understanding of the lead-up to and events of the Battle of Jutland and its significance, the threat posed by the German U-boats, British anti-U-boat measures and their effectiveness, and the importance of the British blockade of Germany.

3

Britain in the war at sea

Events at sea, 1914–15

There were several important events in the North Sea in the early months of the war:

- In August 1914 British destroyers lured German light cruisers out of port near Heligoland Bight and scored an early victory by sinking two of the enemy ships.
- In November and December 1914 the Germans retaliated by launching raids on the British east coast including Scarborough, Whitby and Hartlepool. They caused considerable damage, some civilian deaths, and a blow to the morale of the British people and navy.
- In January 1915 the British cruiser fleet under Admiral Beatty intercepted the German cruiser fleet which intended to destroy the British fishing fleet at Dogger Bank. Several German ships were damaged or sunk and there were no further raids on the British coastline.

The Battle of Jutland, May 1916

- On 31 May 1916 the only major sea battle of the First World War took place at Jutland, just off the coast of Denmark.

- The new German commander, Admiral Scheer, wanted to break the British blockade by sinking some of Britain's cruiser fleet.
- The British cruisers sailed towards Jutland to trap the German fleet. The British had decoded German naval messages and were aware that the German High Seas fleet had also left port.

In the battle which followed:

- The two fleets engaged, with Britain losing three ships because of structural defects.
- The Germans, realising at the last minute that they were sailing into a trap, turned and began to sail back to Germany. They reached safety despite being pursued by the British fleet led by Admiral Jellicoe.

Who won?

Both sides claimed victory:

- The Germans because they had inflicted heavier losses and casualties on the British. (The British lost fourteen ships and 6000 men; the Germans, eleven ships and 2500 men.)
- The British because Scheer had run away from the battle.
- In fact it was a long-term victory for the British. Scheer had failed to break the blockade and the German fleet remained in port for most of the rest of the war. The following year the Germans were forced to gamble on unrestricted U-boat warfare. This brought the USA into the war on the Allied side.

Summary box 1

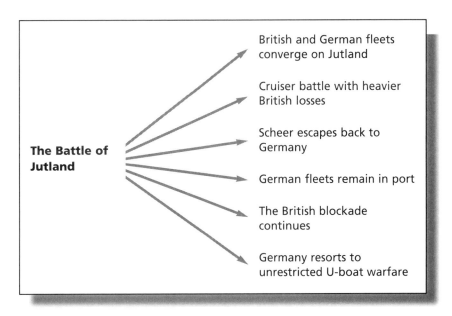

The Battle of Jutland
- British and German fleets converge on Jutland
- Cruiser battle with heavier British losses
- Scheer escapes back to Germany
- German fleets remain in port
- The British blockade continues
- Germany resorts to unrestricted U-boat warfare

Submarine warfare

The Germans decided to use their U-boats (submarines) to try to starve Britain out of the war. Britain was not self-sufficient and had to import food supplies.

Use of U-boats by the Germans

- At first German U-boats attacked only British and Allied ships.
- In February 1915 Germany decided on unrestricted U-boat warfare and sank any ships trading with Britain.
- In May 1915 a German U-boat sank the passenger liner *Lusitania,* killing more than 1000 passengers including over 120 Americans. The USA protested but Germany insisted that the liner was also carrying armaments for Britain.
- After more protests from the USA and other neutral countries, Germany called off unrestricted warfare in August 1915.
- The failure to break the blockade at Jutland forced the Germans to gamble again on unrestricted U-boat warfare in February 1917. The gamble was an attempt to starve Britain out of the war before the USA could make any significant contribution.
- The gamble almost paid off. By May 1917 Britain was down to six weeks' supply of wheat.

Anti-U-boat measures

Nevertheless the German gamble did not work. In April 1917 the USA entered the war on the Allied side. Also, Britain developed a series of anti-U-boat measures:

- Hydrophones, which were used to detect the sound of U-boat engines.
- Depth charges, which exploded under water.
- Q-boats: disguised armed vessels which lured the U-boats to the surface before sinking them.
- The Dover barrage, which consisted of mines and nets from Dover to Calais to try to block the entry of the U-boats through the Channel to the Atlantic.
- The convoy system. This system was introduced in April 1917: merchant ships were escorted by armed vessels equipped with hydrophones and depth charges. This proved the decisive measure: fewer and fewer merchant ships were attacked and sunk, while a growing number of U-boats were destroyed.

Summary box 2

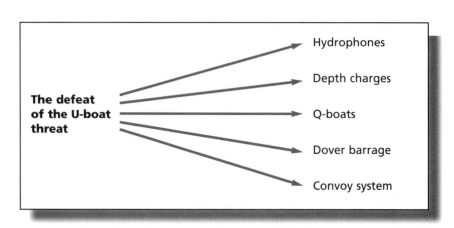

The defeat of the U-boat threat → Hydrophones, Depth charges, Q-boats, Dover barrage, Convoy system

The British blockade

The British navy imposed a long-range blockade of Germany from the very start of the war.

- This was not very effective at first. From 1914 to 1916 Germany still traded with the USA and, overland, got essential dairy supplies from Denmark and iron ore from Sweden.

- The blockade was more effective between 1917 and 1918. The US entry into the war meant trade ceased, and Denmark and Sweden agreed to limit their exports to Germany. By the beginning of 1918 Germany was seriously short of food supplies, which badly affected civilian morale and health. The German war effort was also handicapped by a shortage of iron ore for the manufacture of munitions and chemicals to make poisonous gas.

- The blockade was an important reason for Ludendorff's decision to launch the Spring Offensives of 1918.

...4........................

What do I Know?

What was important about:

- The Battle of Dogger Bank

- The Battle of Jutland

- The sinking of the *Lusitania*

- The convoy system?

1 Where did the British score an early success against the German fleet in August 1914?

2 Where did the German fleet raid in November–December 1914?

3 Name the commanders of the German High Seas fleet and British Grand fleet at the Battle of Jutland.

4 Why did Germany claim victory in this battle?

5 Which passenger liner was sunk by a German U-boat in May 1915?

6 What is meant by 'unrestricted U-boat warfare'?

7 When was the convoy system introduced?

8 What were Q-boats?

9 Which countries limited their exports to Germany, 1917–18?

10 What effects did the British blockade have on the German civilian population?

My score ......

5

Exam Type Question

Here is the sort of source-based question you might be asked in an exam paper. Look closely at the answers given and the examiner's comments on them. Then answer the practice question.

▼ **Headline from a British newspaper four days after the Battle of Jutland.**

JUNE 4, 1916   SUNDAY PICTORIAL   PAGE 3

GROWING TOLL OF ENEMY LOSSES IN THE SEA BATTLE

Majority of the German Light Cruisers and Destroyers Reported Lost.

FLOTILLA DRIVEN INTO THEIR OWN MINEFIELD

How Airships and Airmen Scouts Helped the German Fleet—20 Torpedo Boats Gone.

THREE ZEPPELINS BROUGHT DOWN.

Only two brief official communiqués on the North Sea battle were issued last night. Neither adds anything further to the details of the fight.

One corrects German lies about our losses and the other gives a brief summary of our casualties among officers. Admiral Beatty is reported to be unharmed.

A dramatic statement last night was that the German destroyer and light cruiser flotilla were driven into their own minefield and the majority of them lost. The survivors speak of at least twenty torpedo craft as among their "colossal" losses.

The outstanding fact is that the German Fleet—" the whole German fleet "—emerged from its Canal on " an enterprise directed towards the North." It failed in its purpose; and when the British " main forces " appeared on the scene, fled back to its base.

Yesterday three Zeppelins were reported destroyed in the battle—two shot down over the sea and one wrecked just as she got back to Germany.

WARSPITE IN PORT.

Official Denial of German Admiralty Lies.

PRESS BUREAU, Saturday.
The Secretary of the Admiralty makes the following announcement :—
With reference to the German wireless message to the Embassy, Washington, to-day, containing a report of the speech of the President of the Reichstag, it is noted that the loss of the battleship Warspite is again officially affirmed.

ZEPPELINS HELP FOE.

Von Scheer in Command of All Available German Forces.

AMSTERDAM, Saturday.
A semi-official telegram from Berlin says:—
In the naval battle in the Skagerack the Chief of the Fleet, Vice-Admiral von Scheer, was in command of the German forces, which consisted of the German High Sea Fleet with Dreadnoughts, older ships

"WE ARE THE GAINERS."

Mr. Churchill on the Admirals' Reports on the Sea Fight.

THE BLOW TO THE ENEMY.

Mr. Winston Churchill, who has had the privilege of examining the reports of the admirals and of considering the information in the possession of the Admiralty, says :—
" The naval supremacy of the British Fleet in capital ships depends upon the super-Dreadnoughts armed with the 13.5in. and 15in. guns, and these are sufficient by themselves to maintain control of the seas.
" Of these vital units of the first rank we have only lost one—the Queen Mary. There appears to be no doubt that the Germans have lost at least one comparable ship.
" If this should be the Lutzow or the Derfflinger, that vessel is the heavier loss to them, actually and relatively, than the Queen Mary is to us.
" The sinking of the two brand new German light cruisers, Wiesbaden and Elbing, is, in fact, a more grievous loss to the enemy. In all those vessels the most serious feature is the loss of their splendid and irreplacable crews.
" The destroyer casualties appear to be about equal. On these terms, we, being the stronger, are the gainers.
" Our margin of superiority is in no way impaired. The dispatch of troops to the Continent should continue with the utmost freedom, the battered condition of the German Fleet being an additional security to us.
" The hazy weather, the fall of night, and the retreat of the enemy alone frustrated the persevering efforts of our brilliant commanders, Sir John Jellicoe and Sir David Beatty, to force a final decision.

THE KING'S MESSAGE.

"Many Personal Friends of My Own Have Fallen."

OUR LINE PIERCED IN BIG ATTACK.

Germans' 700 Yards Gain on Ypres Front.

TWO GENERALS MISSING.

Canadian Counter - Attacks Regain Much Lost Ground.

(BRITISH OFFICIAL.)

GENERAL HEADQUARTERS, Saturday, 10.19 p.m.
Fighting of a very severe nature has continued without cessation south-east of Ypres, between Hooge and Ypres-Menin Railway.
Following on their initial advantage obtained yesterday evening in penetrating our forward line in this neighbourhood, the Germans pushed their attacks during the night and succeeded in pushing through our defences to a depth of 700 yards in the direction of Zillebeke.
The Canadian troops, however, who are holding this sector of the defences, launched counter-strokes at 7 a.m. this morning which have succeeded gradually in driving the enemy from much of the ground which he had gained.
The Canadians behaved with the utmost gallantry in counter-attacking successfully after a heavy and continuous bombardment.
The enemy losses have been severe, and a large number of German dead have been abandoned on the recaptured ground.
Generals Mercer and Williams, of the 3rd Canadian Division, who were inspecting the front trenches yesterday during the bombardment, are missing.
Opposite the re-entrant of our line near Fricourt, north of the River Somme, a small party of a regiment raided the German trenches last night, bringing back a few prisoners with them. This party had a sharp engagement in the German trench and suffered some casualties, but succeeded in bombing several German dugouts.
South of Angres last night we carried out a successful enterprise. Our party entered a German trench, disposed of the garrison above ground, and bombed five dugouts before return-

---

How useful is the source for explaining the events and results of the Battle of Jutland?   **(8 marks)**

Answer

The source is useful because it tells us that there was a growing toll of enemy losses in the sea battle. It says that the majority of German light cruisers and destroyers were reported lost. It is also useful because it was written only four days after the battle and the newspaper will know what happened.

Examiner's Comments

2 out of 8

The answer accepts the contents of the source at face value and believes that its contents make it useful. The second sentence does give a very basic evaluation – that it is useful because it was written near to the time of the battle. To get full marks the answer would need to evaluate the positive value of the source as propaganda and discuss its purpose, and also consider the limitations of the source as evidence of the Battle of Jutland.

6

Practice Question

Now try to answer this sort of question yourself.

▼ **An artist's impression of the sinking of the *Lusitania*.**

How useful is the source for showing the sinking of the *Lusitania* in May 1915? **(8 marks)**

Remember that to answer a question on usefulness you need to write a balanced answer:

1 What is useful about the source?
- Does it give important or relevant information about the event?
- Does it give a unique or different view?
- Is it by someone whose view is worth knowing or would have insight into what was happening?
- Is it a good example of propaganda or a biased view?

2 What are the limitations of the source?
- What information is missing from the source? Is this information vital?
- Is the source strongly biased; does it give only one view or a limited view?
- Does the source exaggerate or distort what took place?
- How reliable is the author of the source?

3 Remember to write a fair amount. This question is worth 8 marks.

2.3 How did the First World War change life in Britain?

1 Topic Summary

The First World War was the first 'total war'. That is, it was the first war to include civilians as well as the military in the day-to-day events. The British population was greatly affected by censorship and propaganda, recruitment, particularly conscription, and greater government control including rationing. Perhaps the greatest impact was on the position of women.

2 What do I Need to Know?

You will need to have a knowledge and understanding of the changing attitudes to the war at home, the use and impact of censorship and propaganda, the effect of air raids and submarine warfare on the civilian population, and greater government control including food rationing, recruitment methods, conscription, and the changing role of women.

3 The First World War and life in Britain

Changing attitudes at home
In August 1914 there was great enthusiasm for the war in Britain:

- In the first few months of the war, over 1 million men volunteered to join the British army.
- Government propaganda convinced the British people of the need to support the war effort. Many believed it would be short-lived and over by Christmas 1914.

This enthusiasm did not last for long. By 1916 there was growing disillusionment and even pessimism about the war. This was due to:

- The failure to achieve a quick victory.
- Increasing awareness of events on the Western Front and the horrors of trench warfare.
- Growing casualty lists especially after the Battle of the Somme.
- The increased impact of the war on the civilian population. By 1917 there were food shortages due to U-boat sinkings. German ships had bombarded the east coast as early as November 1914 and German air raids by Zeppelins and then bombers caused damage and further casualties.

Summary box 1

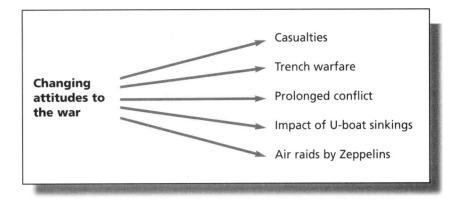

Censorship and propaganda

The government was keen to control what people read, heard and thought. This was in order to keep up morale, ensure support for the war effort and turn people against the enemy:

- The government carefully censored what was written or shown about the war. Newspapers printed official figures and versions, not the horrors of the battles. Reporters were not allowed in the front-line trenches until late in the war. Losses were given as gains and defeats were written up as victories. Even soldiers' letters from the front were censored in order to keep up morale.
- Posters and newspaper stories portrayed the Germans as evil. They were called the 'Huns' after a barbarian tribe of the fifth century. There were newspaper reports that they crucified enemy soldiers, raped nuns and bayoneted babies.

Recruitment

Reliance on volunteers

This was one of the key roles of government during the war. Heavy losses on the Western Front meant that more and more men had to be encouraged or, eventually, forced to join up.

The British army was supplemented by troops from the Empire. Canadian, Australian, New Zealand, Indian and South African troops played a crucial role in the battles of the Western Front.

In 1914 Britain did not have a conscript army and the government encouraged men to volunteer using various methods. Men volunteered for a variety of reasons:

- Patriotism – the belief it was their duty to fight for Britain.
- Hatred of the Germans due to their invasion of 'little' Belgium and the impact of propaganda.
- Guilt: conscience posters made men feel guilty for not joining up.
- War also seemed to promise adventure. For many it was the chance to escape poverty and unemployment.

- Women encouraged men to join up and gave out white feathers (signs of cowardice) to those who did not.
- 'Pals' batallions' encouraged friends from the same street, area, or factory to join up together.
- Kitchener, the Minister of War, organised a famous poster campaign based on 'Your country needs you'.

Summary box 2

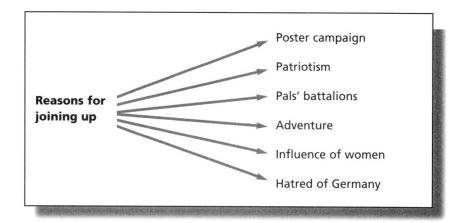

Conscription

By early 1916 the flood of volunteers had begun to dry up as more and more men became aware of the horrors of trench warfare. At the same time losses on the Western Front made recruitment even more of a priority. Therefore, in 1916 the government introduced conscription, at first only for unmarried men, but soon extended to married men.

Some men refused to join up for religious, political or moral reasons. These were known as conscientious objectors and had to face a trial to decide if their views were genuine. Some 'conchies' agreed to drive ambulances or work as stretcher-bearers. About 1500 absolutely refused to have anything to do with the war. They were sent to prison where they were often treated with great cruelty.

Rationing and the effects of submarine warfare

- The government took greater control of everyday life. The Defence of the Realm Act (DORA), introduced in August 1914, was used to censor papers, water down beer, control hours and places of work, and introduce rationing.
- German submarines blockaded Britain's ports and attacked merchant ships carrying food. This policy of unrestricted warfare brought Britain close to starvation and surrender in 1917.
- White bread was banned in 1916 because grain was in short supply. In 1917 people were asked to eat only 1.1 kg of meat a week (the government was not keen to introduce rationing).

- In January 1918 sugar was rationed. By the spring, butter, tea, jam, margarine, meat and bacon had been added to the ration list.
- Not everyone was affected in the same way. The poor often had to queue before dawn to get their share, while the better off were able to buy things on the 'black market'.
- Nevertheless, many of the poorer people were better fed than they had ever been. In poorer areas, food kitchens were set up. Mostly, they served penny portions of food, mainly to children and old age pensioners.

Summary box 3

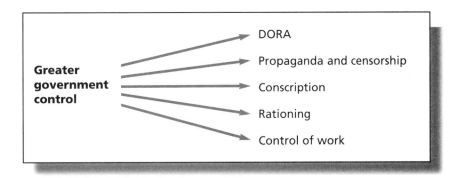

The changing role of women
The war had a dramatic effect on the position of women:

- Before the war women were seen as second-class citizens. Despite various campaigns they were not allowed to vote, had few employment opportunities and were poorly paid.
- Women were needed and encouraged to take over the jobs of men who had joined up. Their role in factories, as nurses and in food production became essential for victory. About 15,000 women joined the Voluntary Aid Detachments (VADs), serving behind the lines to look after casualties.
- Many worked in munitions factories making the shells for the Western Front. This was unpleasant and dangerous work.
- The women's armed forces were set up, including the Women's Royal Naval Service (WRNS) and the Women's Army Auxiliary Corps (WAAC).
- Women earned more and enjoyed more social freedom. Single women were able to socialise, including drinking and smoking, without a chaperone. They wore shorter skirts – even trousers – and had their hair cut short.
- As a result of their efforts women were rewarded with the vote in the Representation of the People Act of 1918. This Act gave the vote to all men aged 21 or over but only to women aged over 30. Women were also given greater opportunities in careers such as the legal profession and the civil service.
- There were, however, drawbacks. Most women had to give up their new jobs when men returned from the front and either go back to the home or their traditional employment.

4 What do I Know?

What was important about:
- Propaganda
- Censorship
- Rationing
- DORA
- Conscription?

1 Give two reasons for enthusiasm for the war in 1914.
2 What did the government censor?
3 What name did the newspapers give to the Germans?
4 What were conscience posters?
5 What were 'pals' battalions'?
6 Why was conscription introduced in 1916?
7 What name was given to those men who refused to join up?
8 What does DORA stand for?
9 What was the first food to be rationed?
10 What does WAAC stand for?

My score ......

5 Exam Type Question

Here is the sort of source-based question you might be asked in an exam paper. Look closely at the answer given and the examiner's comments on it. Then answer the practice question.

Source A

One of the most revolutionary changes of the war was the participation of women in the war effort. The upper-class women benefited most by being freed from a pointless life of tea-parties and gossip. The war gave women the chance to use their abilities and to obtain equality as citizens. In Britain they obtained in 1918 the vote for women over 30.

▲ From *World War I* by Dudley Woodget, 1976.

Is Source A a fair interpretation of the impact of the First World War on the position of women in Britain? Use Source A and your own knowledge to answer the question.

(8 marks)

Answer

Source A appears to be a fair interpretation. It was written by an historian in 1976 with the benefit of hindsight, able to see the more long-term effects of the war on the position of women. In addition he will have been able to consult a variety of sources and should be trying to be as objective as possible. The participation of women in the war effort was certainly revolutionary because they undertook jobs which had been exclusively for men, especially in heavy industry. They were rewarded with the vote in 1918.

However, the interpretation is not totally fair. Woodget seems to exaggerate the effects of the war, possibly in order to promote the progress made by women during the war, and generalises its impact. The war did not give the chance for women to achieve equality but simply to improve their existing lowly position. He fails to mention that although women over 30 got the vote, this was not equality because the vote was given to men over 21. In addition women had to give up most of the jobs they had undertaken when the men returned from the front. There were few gains in employment opportunities.

Examiner's Comments

7 out of 8

An excellent answer. It gives a balanced evaluation of the interpretation by discussing the purpose and situation of the author and using own knowledge to discuss the accuracy of what the historian has written.

6

Practice Question

Now try to answer this sort of question yourself.

Source B

> The world and women had changed. Some of the sillier ideas about women had gone for good. For determined women there were totally new professional opportunities. The war also changed the way women thought about themselves: women who went back to domestic service and shop work insisted on much better conditions than they had before the war.

▲ From *Women at War* by A Marwick, 1977.

Is Source B an accurate interpretation of the progress made by women as a result of the First World War? Use Source B and your own knowledge to answer the question. **(8 marks)**

Refer to page 65 for hints on answering this kind of source-based question.

3 Britain in the Second World War

3.1 Britain's role in the war against Germany, 1939–41

Topic Summary

In 1939 Europe went to war. Within a year Britain 'stood alone' against Germany as Hitler's armies overran Norway, Denmark, Belgium, Holland and France. British armies retreated to the port of Dunkirk where they were rescued by the combined efforts of the British navy and RAF. Britain survived for the next year because of the leadership qualities of Winston Churchill, support from the USA, success in the Battle of Britain and the resolve created by the Blitz.

What do I Need to Know?

You should have a knowledge and understanding of *Blitzkrieg* (lightning war) and the reasons for early German success in 1939–40, the 'phoney war' and the failure to save Norway, and the events of May–June 1940 which brought the defeat of France. You should also know about Dunkirk and whether it was a success or failure, and Britain's survival 1940–41, especially the leadership of Churchill, the Battle of Britain and the Blitz.

Britain's role against Germany

Early German success, 1939–40

On 3 September 1939 Britain and France declared war on Germany. As with the First World War, the British immediately sent the BEF to support the French. Nevertheless, within nine months Hitler had conquered most of Western Europe:

- In September 1939 German forces invaded Poland and within two weeks had captured the country.
- During the next six months nothing much happened in a period known as the 'phoney war'. Britain and France remained on the defensive, believing that France's defence system - the Maginot Line - would stop any German attacks.
- In April 1940 Hitler's armies invaded Norway and Denmark. Two British expeditions failed to prevent the fall of Norway. The British Prime Minister, Neville Chamberlain, resigned and was replaced by Winston Churchill.

Reasons for early German success

- The Germans had only one commander, Hitler, while the Allies were divided among several leaders.
- *Blitzkrieg* was a new method of fighting which took the enemy by surprise. The Germans attacked at speed the weaker part of the enemy defences using dive bombers, paratroopers, armoured vehicles and tanks. They achieved quick breathroughs and outflanked the enemy's defences.
- The Allies were not prepared for *Blitzkrieg*. Britain and France made few preparations during the period of the 'phoney war', preferring to wait behind the Maginot Line. They scattered their tanks instead of concentrating them against German operations.
- The Germans outflanked the Maginot Line and attacked the weakest part of France's border, the Ardennes, a heavily wooded area which the French believed was inaccessible to tanks.
- Britain refused to commit many planes and tanks to the defence of France in case of French defeat and a German invasion.

Summary box 1

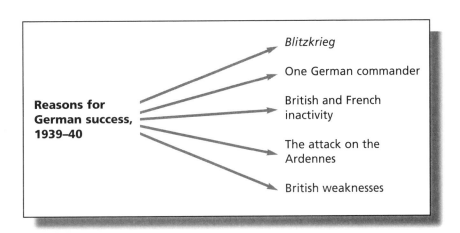

Reasons for German success, 1939–40
- Blitzkrieg
- One German commander
- British and French inactivity
- The attack on the Ardennes
- British weaknesses

Dunkirk, May–June 1940

The British troops in France supporting the French forces were pushed back to the port of Dunkirk. For nine days between 27 May and 4 June, the *Luftwaffe* (the German air force) pounded the beaches as the Royal Navy evacuated men back to England. The evacuation was achieved through:

- Hundreds of small, privately-owned boats that went to the beaches of Dunkirk to rescue as many troops as possible and transfer them to bigger Royal Navy vessels waiting off shore.
- The protection given by the Royal Navy.
- The support of the RAF which attacked the *Luftwaffe* and prevented heavy casualties on the beaches of Dunkirk.
- The BEF rearguard, who stayed behind and sacrificed their freedom or lives to hold back the German attackers.
- Hitler's failure to use tanks at Dunkirk.

Dunkirk: a success?

Winston Churchill claimed that Dunkirk was a great British success story. He referred to it as a miracle:

- He aroused the 'Dunkirk spirit' to keep up the morale of the British people.
- The British government hoped that at least 50,000 men could be rescued. In fact, it was an even bigger success: around 340,000 were rescued in Operation Dynamo (the evacuation from Dunkirk).

Dunkirk: a disaster?

Dunkirk was, in most respects, a disaster for the BEF:

- The British army had been forced to retreat in the face of *Blitzkrieg*.
- Huge amounts of military equipment had to be abandoned, including 475 tanks, 1000 heavy guns and 400 anti-tank guns.
- The defeat of France followed soon after. Britain was now alone in the face of a possible German invasion.

Britain alone, 1940–41

Britain now faced Germany alone. It survived the next year thanks to:

- The leadership of Winston Churchill. He made stirring speeches in which he insisted that Britain would never surrender. He kept up the morale of the British people with his bulldog spirit.
- American aid. Even though the USA was neutral, President Roosevelt agreed to send essential supplies to Britain through a 'lend–lease' system which enabled Britain to pay for goods at a later date.
- The Battle of Britain. Hitler wanted to invade Britain, but he knew he could not succeed until he had destroyed the RAF. Between July and September 1940, the RAF and *Luftwaffe* fought the Battle of Britain in the skies over Britain. By early September Hitler was close to defeating the RAF. In the first week, the British lost 185 aircraft and 300 airmen, more than could be quickly replaced. But then, on 7 September 1940, he switched tactics and, instead of military targets, he concentrated on night-time air raids on Britain's cities known as the Blitz. Hitler had made the mistake of diverting attacks from the airfields to the cities, and this marked the end of the Battle of Britain.
- The Blitz aimed to destroy the morale of the British people by attacking homes, transport and industry. It continued until the summer of 1941, by which time 43,000 British people had been killed. The worst single air raid was on Coventry on 14 November 1940 when 4000 people were killed.

- However, the Blitz made the British people even more determined to carry on fighting the war against Hitler.
- British strengths included a defence system based on radar. In addition, the British fighters – the Spitfire and the Hurricane – were superior to their German counterparts.
- British bombing attacks on Germany first took place in 1940. Initially, strategic targets were bombed but, by 1942, whole cities – particularly in the Ruhr industrial region – were being bombed. This tactic was an attempt to break Germany's military strength and the people's morale.
- Finally Britain was saved by Hitler's decision to invade Russia. Operation Barbarossa was launched on 22 June 1941. Hitler diverted his planes, tanks and other resources from Western Europe in the attempt to defeat and conquer the Soviet Union.

Summary box 2

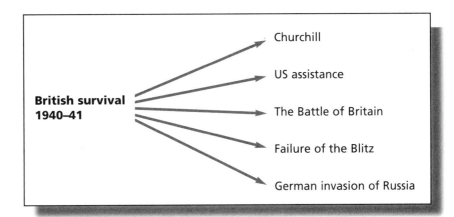

British survival 1940–41
- Churchill
- US assistance
- The Battle of Britain
- Failure of the Blitz
- German invasion of Russia

4

What do I Know?

1 What was *Blitzkrieg*?

2 What was the 'phoney war'?

3 Which countries did Hitler invade in April 1940?

4 Why were the French defences weak in the Ardennes area?

5 Give one reason for Hitler's successes of 1939–40.

6 Who resigned as British Prime Minister in April 1940?

7 What was 'lend-lease'?

8 Name the British fighter planes used during the Battle of Britain.

9 What was the name of the early warning device used by Britain during this battle?

10 Which British city was bombed on 14 November 1940?

My score ......

What was important about:
- *Blitzkrieg*
- Winston Churchill
- Dunkirk
- The Battle of Britain
- The Blitz?

5

Exam Type Question

Here are the sort of source-based questions you might be asked in an exam paper. Look closely at the answers given and the examiner's comments on them. Then answer the practice question.

Source A

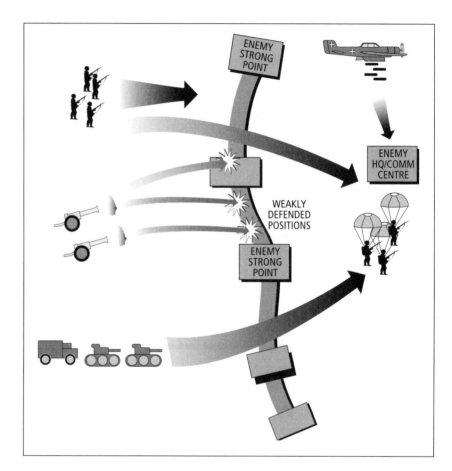

▲ German *Blitzkrieg* tactics in the Second World War.

> What does Source A suggest about how *Blitzkrieg* tactics
> were used by the Germans in 1939–40?   **(3 marks)**

Answer

The diagram shows us the various stages of Blitzkrieg. First the Germans dropped parachutists behind enemy lines. They then attacked the enemy defences using dive bombers. Finally they drove through with great speed using armoured cars, tanks and motorised infantry.

Examiner's Comments

3 out of 3
A very good answer. It has managed to make at least three significant interpretations of how the Germans used *Blitzkrieg* in 1939-40.

Source B

> The first day of the evacuation, 27 May, proved disappointing. Only 7669 troops were brought out by a motley assortment of destroyers, passenger ferry steamers, paddle steamers, self-propelled barges and Dutch schuits. Later a volunteer Armada of some 400 yachts, lifeboats, launches, river tugs, cockle boats, pleasure craft, French and Belgian fishing boats and oyster dredgers ferried 100,000 men from the beaches on 30 May.

▲ From *Memoirs of Dunkirk* by S Webb.

> Source B explains one reason for the success of the Dunkirk evacuation. Using Source B and your own knowledge, explain why most Allied troops were evacuated from the beaches of Dunkirk.   **(6 marks)**

Answer

One reason for the success was because, as it says in Source B, there were so many boats that went across to Dunkirk. Another reason was because the RAF protected the men on the beaches. It was also successful because Hitler did not send tanks to Dunkirk to force a way through.

Examiner's Comments

3 out of 6
This gives three reasons for the success in evacuating troops from Dunkirk, including one from Source B. Unfortunately, none of the reasons are fully explained and developed. Therefore, this answer would only score half marks.

6

Practice Question

Now try to answer this sort of question yourself.

Source C

> The British expedition was dumped into Norway's deep snows and quagmires of April slush without a single anti-aircraft gun, without one squadron of supporting airplanes and without a single piece of artillery. There were neither snow-shoes nor skis, still less skiers.

▲ From the *Chicago Daily News*, April 1940.

What does Source C tell us about the reasons for the failure of the British Norwegian expedition in April 1940? **(3 marks)**

Remember that for this type of question:

1 You need to pick out three factors because you will be given a mark for each relevant point.

2 Do not write too much. This question is worth only 3 marks.

Source D

> The bombing campaign has had the least effect of all, so far as we can see, on the morale and will to resist of the British people. No decisive success can be expected from terror attacks on residential areas.

▲ From Hitler's war directive against England, 6 February 1941.

Source D gives one reason for the failure of the Blitz. Using Source D and your own knowledge, explain why the German attempts to bomb Britain, 1940–41, were not successful. **(6 marks)**

Remember that for this question:

1 You need to fully explain at least two reasons. Write a paragraph for each.

2 One reason should lead from the source and one from your own knowledge.

3.2 Britain's contribution to the defeat of Germany, 1941–45

...1...

Topic Summary

Having survived alone from 1940 to 1941, Britain gained two formidable allies in the Soviet Union and the USA. This became known as the Grand Alliance. From 1942 the British and the US began preparations for an invasion of France which eventually took place in June 1944. The D-Day landings proved successful and were followed by a slow advance through France and the Low Countries. Britain, however, also had to survive one other serious threat: German use of U-boats to try to starve the British out of the war. This was known as the Battle of the Atlantic.

...2...

What do I Need to Know?

You will be expected to have a thorough knowledge of the Battle of the Atlantic and the threats posed by the U-boats and measures used to combat them, the preparations for and success of the D-Day landings of 1944, and the Allied advance, 1944–45. You will also need to understand the reasons for the defeat of Germany.

...3...

Britain and the defeat of Germany, 1941–45

The Battle of the Atlantic

Germany had almost won the First World War by cutting off Britain's supplies from the USA using unrestricted U-boat warfare. Germany used the same tactics at the start of the Second World War and, at first, was very successful. By mid-1941 so many ships were being sunk that the British government stopped publishing the figures. In 1941, 1299 Allied ships were sunk (six times as many as could be replaced) but only 87 U-boats were sunk (the Germans could easily replace these losses). By July 1942, U-boats were being launched at the rate of 30 a month and sank 1700 Allied ships.

Early U-boat success

- The U-boats were successful because they used new tactics. They hunted in 'wolf packs' and usually attacked at night while operating on the surface. This meant they could not be detected by ASDIC, the allied device for finding U-boats under the water.
- Britain did use the convoy system but the Royal Navy had few destroyers available to escort convoys and provide them with cover. Whenever possible the U-boats attacked unescorted ships or 'stragglers' unable to keep up with the convoys.

End of the U-boat threat

The turning-point in the Battle of the Atlantic was May 1943 when the Allies sank 41 U-boats, and that year the Germans lost almost 300 U-boats. At the same time the number of sinkings of Allied ships gradually fell. The U-boat threat was defeated by several developments:

- The USA was able to launch ships much faster than the U-boats could sink them.
- Aircraft were used as escorts for the convoys and were very successful in locating and attacking U-boats.
- The convoys were given more escort vessels. In order to locate the U-boats, the vessels used radar.
- The Allies were able to decode German U-boat messages and work out the location of the U-boats.

The D-Day landings

On 6 June 1944 British and US troops landed in Normandy as part of Operation Overlord. The invasion of France had been planned since 1942 but, despite Soviet pressure to invade earlier, Churchill and Roosevelt were determined to be properly prepared. The Allies landed on five beaches each given a code-name – the British on 'Gold', 'Juno' and 'Sword' and the Americans on 'Utah' and 'Omaha'. By nightfall over 150,000 soldiers had landed. About 3600 British and Canadian soldiers were killed or wounded; there were about 6000 US casualties, the majority at Omaha. But over the next two days the Allies established their positions and moved inland to liberate France.

Success of Operation Overlord

Operation Overlord was a success for several reasons:

- Thorough Allied preparations. Soldiers had been in training for many months and had practised landing techniques.
- The US General, Dwight D Eisenhower, was made overall Supreme Commander of D-Day and did much to unite the armies of each country.
- Normandy was carefully chosen because it had ideal beaches for landing troops.
- The Allies deliberately confused the Germans over where the landings would take place. The Germans believed it would be a French port such as Calais or Dieppe and heavily reinforced these areas. The Allies bombed these areas to convince the Germans that this was where the landings would take place.
- There was total secrecy. The British soldiers who set off for France did not know where the landings would take place.
- On the day of the invasion Hitler refused to believe that the landings in Normandy were genuine. He was convinced they were a decoy from Calais. His delay in sending reinforcements gave the Allies the chance to establish a bridgehead.

Summary box 2

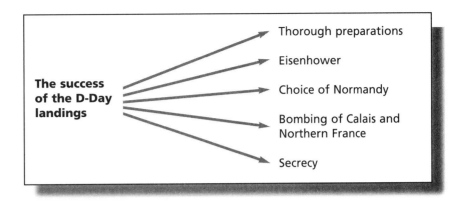

The success of the D-Day landings
- Thorough preparations
- Eisenhower
- Choice of Normandy
- Bombing of Calais and Northern France
- Secrecy

The defeat of Germany, 1944–45

Over the next nine months the Allies advanced slowly through France and the Low Countries to Germany.

- Having liberated France in August, the Allies reached the River Rhine by September and set about capturing bridges held by the Germans. They met with some resistance from retreating German forces.
- In December 1944 Hitler made one final attack. He launched an offensive in the Ardennes in what became known as the Battle of the Bulge. This battle delayed the Allied advance by several weeks but, as German fuel supplies dried up, the German advance stopped.
- The German line quickly crumbled and, by the beginning of February, the Germans were in retreat. As German troops retreated out of Western Europe, Soviet forces moved in from the East.
- At the same time Allied bombing of German cities was stepped up. Attacks were made on cities such as Dresden, killing about 25,000 civilians. German transport and industry were severely damaged by the bombings. This contributed to the final defeat of Germany. By the end of the war approximately 600,000 German civilians had been killed in air raids.
- On 30 April 1945 Hitler committed suicide and on 7 May Eisenhower accepted the unconditional surrender of the Germans.

Reasons for German defeat

- Germany was fighting a war on several fronts from 1941, including those against the Soviet Union in the East and Britain in North Africa.
- The success of the D-Day landings meant that Germany was fighting on three fronts: the Soviets in the East, and the British and US in the West and South.
- Germany also faced attack from the skies. British and US bombers carried out massive raids which caused terrible destruction in German cities such as Cologne, Hamburg and Dresden.

4

What do I Know?

What was important about:

- U-boat success in the Atlantic, 1939–43
- Allied victory in the Battle of the Atlantic, 1943–45
- Allied preparations for D-Day
- The D-Day landings?

1 What was ASDIC?

2 Give one reason for the early success of the U-boats.

3 Give one reason for Allied victory in the Battle of the Atlantic.

4 Why did the Allies choose Normandy for the D-Day landings?

5 Give one reason for the success of the D-Day landings.

6 What were the consequences of Allied air attacks on Germany?

7 On what date did Germany finally surrender?

My score ......

5

Exam Type Question

Here is the sort of source-based question you might be asked in an exam paper. Look closely at the answer given and the examiner's comments on it. Then answer the practice question.

▼ **Newspaper headlines for D-Day, 6 June 1944.**

Source A

How useful is Source A for explaining the events of the D-Day landings, June 1944? **(8 marks)**

Answer

Source A is useful because it provides evidence of the D-Day landings. The headlines are accurate in that the Allies did use a considerable number of ships and aircraft to support the landings and, by the end of the first day, establish a beachhead. It is also a good example of the information that newspapers were allowed to publish, showing Allied successes. The reporter may well have accompanied the Allied forces and seen what took place.

Examiner's Comments

5 out of 8

This answer explains the positive value of the source by comparing its contents to own knowledge and looking at the situation in which it was written. However, the answer does lack balance. There is no explanation of the limitations of the source. For example, if the reporter went on the landings how much would he or she have witnessed? Was the news censored? There is also no mention of heavy US casualties on Omaha beach.

6

Practice Question

Now try to answer this sort of question yourself.

Source B

▼ Photograph of the D-Day landings at Omaha Beach in June 1944.

How useful is Source B for showing the D-Day landings of June 1944? **(8 marks)**

Remember that to answer a question on usefulness you need to write a balanced answer. For hints on answering source based questions look back at page 65.

3.3 How did the Second World War change life in Britain?

1

Topic Summary

The Second World War was the second example of 'total war' and had an even greater impact on the civilian population than the First World War. Conscription was introduced when war broke out, as was evacuation. Thousands of children and many mothers and teachers were evacuated from the urban centres to the countryside to escape enemy bombing. The British people had to survive the Blitz and follow a variety of air-raid precautions. The success of the German U-boat campaign meant food shortages and rationing. Once again women played an important role in the war effort.

2

What do I Need to Know?

You will need to have a thorough knowledge of conscription, and the reasons for and effects of evacuation, censorship and propaganda. You will also need to know about the Blitz and air-raid precautions, internment, the role of women, and rationing and the effects of U-boat warfare.

3

The Second World War and life in Britain

Conscription

The government introduced conscription five months before the war began. All men aged between 18 and 40 were conscripted for military service. By 1941, 2 million men had joined the armed forces. Only men in reserved occupations (those vital to the war effort such as coalmining and the fire service) were excused from service.

Evacuation

On 1–3 September 1939, even before Britain declared war on Germany, over 1.5 million people (mainly children) were evacuated from London and other industrial cities to the countryside where they were billeted (stayed) in local homes.

Advantages of evacuation

- It kept children away from the towns and cities that were later bombed.
- It focused attention on poverty in the city slums because people in the country were shocked to see some children suffering from a lack of nutrition, clothing and cleanliness. It brought about demands for reform to alleviate such social problems.
- Some evacuees were well looked after and enjoyed their experiences, working on farms and eating better than they had done before.

Disadvantages of evacuation

- Some evacuees were badly treated by their foster parents and/or became homesick and never really settled in their new surroundings.
- The evacuation process was not well organised. When evacuees arrived in villages they were herded into village halls where they were 'selected' by their foster parents. The dirtiest or least desirable children were often left until last.
- Because of the 'phoney war' many children returned home by Christmas 1939 despite a government poster campaign to prevent them; they had to be re-evacuated later.

Censorship and propaganda

Censorship and propaganda were important:

- They kept up the morale of the British people.
- They ensured that British people supported the war and opposed Germany.
- It was important that the British people did not hear too much 'bad' news, especially during a period of defeat such as 1940–41.

Methods

- Government officials checked written and printed materials, films and photographs to ensure that they contained nothing that might aid the enemy.
- The Ministry of Information kept the public informed about the war and kept up morale. Its early posters were uninspiring and sometimes misinterpreted and did not always create a positive mood.
- As the war progressed, radio, cinema and newspapers all became essential tools for the government. They were used to maintain morale among the British people, so they would fight on with determination.
- The Ministry made use of propaganda campaigns such as 'Dig for victory' and 'Careless talk costs lives'.
- Churchill used radio broadcasts to keep up morale. These were particularly important during the period 1940 to 1941 when Britain stood alone against Germany. He helped to create the 'Dunkirk spirit' and convince people that Dunkirk was a great British success.

Summary box 1

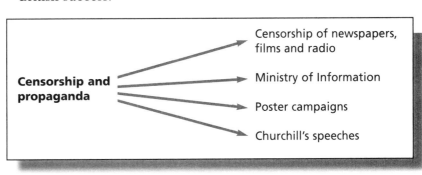

Censorship and propaganda
- Censorship of newspapers, films and radio
- Ministry of Information
- Poster campaigns
- Churchill's speeches

The Blitz

The first major air raids began on London in September 1940. The main targets were the industrial areas and docks. Other towns and cities were bombed, including Coventry, Bristol, Liverpool, Southampton, Birmingham, Manchester and Sheffield. By the end of the Blitz in the summer of 1941, about 43,000 people had been killed and 2 million had been made homeless.

Government measures

The government brought in a variety of measures to deal with air raids and the possibility of a German invasion. These included:

- Evacuation (see p. 84–85).
- The Home Guard. These were Local Defence Volunteers introduced in 1940 as a second line of defence against a possible German invasion. They consisted of men either too old or too young to fight in the army. By June 1940 nearly 1.5 million had joined the Home Guard.
- Air-raid shelters were given out to most homes; the Anderson shelter and the Morrison shelter were the two main types. In London, tube stations were also used as shelters at night. People were given gas-masks to protect themselves against gas attacks.
- Measures were also taken to protect towns against bombers. Government blackout regulations said that every window had to be blacked-out at night. Air Raid Wardens patrolled the streets to check that no lights were visible. Motorists had to use only one headlight and none at all during an air raid.

Internment

There was a worry that there were lots of secret spies in Britain. Soon after the war started, German citizens living in Britain were arrested and put in prisoner-of-war camps – even though some had fled Germany to escape Nazism. By the summer of 1941 the scare had died down, and only about 5000 were kept in prison.

Summary box 2

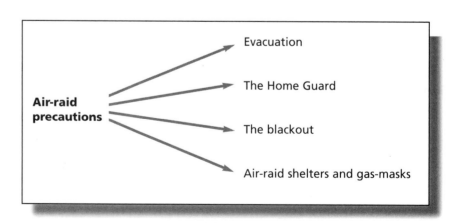

The role of women

In September 1939, as most men of working age were called up for military service, there was a shortage of labour: women were encouraged to fill the jobs that men had left. At first women were encouraged to volunteer but after 1941 the government said that women between 18 and 40 (except those with young children) had to work in war industries. From December 1941, women between 20 and 30 could be conscripted into the armed forces – though not for fighting. Women helped the war effort in various ways:

- On the land, the Women's Land Army, which numbered 80,000 by 1944, made up for the shortage of farm workers.
- They became members of the Women's Royal Naval Services (WRNS), the Women's Army Auxiliary Air Force (WAAF) and Auxiliary Territorial Service (ATS). By 1944 there were 450,000 women working in these three services. Many women worked as mechanics, welders, pilots, carpenters and gunners on anti-aircraft guns. They also worked as nurses, supporting the men on the front line.
- Women played a key role in industry, especially the heavy engineering jobs previously done by men. They worked in munitions factories, the shipyards and in all forms of transport.

Summary box 3

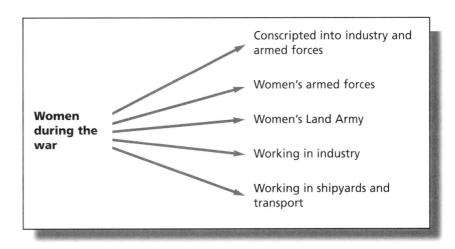

Food shortages and rationing

Before the Second World War, Britain imported over half of its food. However, once the war started, German U-boats began sinking ships bringing essential supplies such as food, clothing, metal and oil to Britain. This quickly led to shortages. The government introduced a variety of measures to deal with these shortages:

- Rationing was introduced in January 1940. Ration books containing coupons were issued and the prices of rationed goods controlled.

- People could not buy rationed goods wherever they wanted: they had to use the shopkeeper where they were registered. The shopkeeper received supplies according to how many customers had registered at the shop. At first only butter, sugar and bacon were rationed. By 1941 other items, such as clothes and petrol, were also included.
- People were encouraged to use alternatives to rationed goods. Some goods came from abroad, such as powdered milk and Spam (Supply Pressed American Meat) from the USA.
- Poster campaigns encouraged people not to waste food and to grow their own vegetables. The 'Dig for Victory' and 'Grow your Own' campaigns were very successful. The number of allotments increased from 815,000 in 1939 to 1.4 million in 1943.
- People also bought food supplies on the 'black market'. These goods were sold at high prices either by traders or 'under the counter' by shopkeepers.

Summary box 4

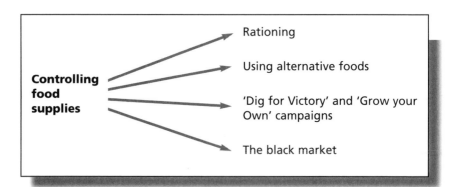

Controlling food supplies → Rationing

Using alternative foods

'Dig for Victory' and 'Grow your Own' campaigns

The black market

4

What do I Know?

What was important about:
- Evacuation
- Conscription
- Propaganda
- The role of women
- Rationing?

1 Why were children and mothers evacuated?
2 Give one criticism of evacuation.
3 When was conscription introduced?
4 Why did the government introduce censorship?
5 What organisation controlled propaganda?
6 Name one of the two main types of air-raid shelter.
7 Why were German nationals interned during the war?
8 What was the name of the organisation that recruited women to work on the land?
9 What was the 'black market'?
10 Name one of the first foods to be rationed.

My score ......

...5..............................

Exam Type Question

Here is the sort of source-based question you might be asked in an exam paper. Look closely at the answer given and the examiner's comments on it. Then answer the practice question.

Source A

Evacuation was not always successful. Some children had a miserable time. Others were resented as a burden by their foster families. They also missed their own families, far away in the cities. Many country families, unaware of how city slum people lived, were in for a shock. They had to deal with children who wet their beds and children who had no experience of a knife and fork to eat with.

▲ From *Modern World History* by T Hewitt, J McCabe and A Mendum, 1999.

Is Source A a fair interpretation of the effects of evacuation during the Second World War? Use Source A and your own knowledge to answer the question. **(8 marks)**

Answer

Source A appears to be a fair interpretation. It was written by historians who, in 1999, had the benefit of hindsight and were able to consult a variety of sources and views about evacuation. They should be as objective as possible in their research and conclusions. Some children were certainly homesick and had returned home by Christmas 1939. Others were treated badly by foster parents only interested in the money. Some evacuees had a miserable existence.

However, the interpretation is not totally fair. The three historians only give one side of evacuation. For some evacuees life in the countryside was far more pleasant than the slums they came from. Some foster parents treated them well and they were far healthier and better fed than they had been in the towns and cities. The textbook highlights the worst aspects of evacuation possibly because these are of more interest to students of the Second World War.

Examiner's Comments

7 out of 8
A very good answer. It gives a balanced evaluation of the interpretation by discussing the purpose and situation of the authors and using own knowledge to discuss the accuracy of what has been written.

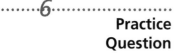

Practice Question

Source B

Now try to answer this sort of question yourself.

> There were many who believed that the traditional jobs were the only ones women were capable of doing. The commonly held attitudes that women could only perform simple tasks and that certain jobs were unglamorous or not feminine were difficult to change. Indeed, many women when interviewed during the war were happy to say they were looking forward to giving up their jobs, marrying and having children.

▲ **From *Modern World History* by M Chandler and JW Wright, 1999.**

Is Source B a fair interpretation of the effects of the Second World War on the position of women in Britain? Use Source B and your own knowledge to answer the question. **(8 marks)**

Remember to do the following:

1 Give a balanced answer which looks at what is accurate and not so accurate or fair.
  • Compare what has been written to what you know.
  • Is it accurate? Has the author missed out important developments?
  • Is the author biased and does he or she exaggerate?

2 Examine the purpose/motives/situation of the author to see if this affects fairness and accuracy.
  • Is the author objective or trying to make you think a certain way or prove a particular point of view?

3 Write a reasonably detailed answer. This question is worth 8 marks.

4 Russia/the USSR, 1914–41

4.1 The end of Tsarism, 1914–17

...1

Topic Summary

In 1900 Russia was a huge, economically backward country. Its ruler, Nicholas II, governed as an autocrat with complete control. All political opposition to him was crushed. However, in the period up to 1914, revolutionary groups emerged. After a revolution in 1905 the Tsar was forced to set up a Duma (Parliament). This had only limited powers and the Tsar's control remained strong. Then, in 1914, Russia went to war. All the weaknesses in Russia – political, military, economic – were exposed. The result was another revolution in March 1917. This one forced the Tsar to abdicate.

...2

What do I Need to Know?

There are two key issues that you need to understand. The first is the strength of the Tsar's rule in 1914 – the total control the Tsar had over Russia. You also need to appreciate the changes that had taken place – there was more opposition to the Tsar's rule and a Duma had been set up. The second issue is the collapse of the Tsar's rule in the relatively short time span of 1914 to 1917. Here you will need to understand the effects of the war on Russia: how weaknesses in the government and army, and shortages of food, created a backlash that brought about a revolution that overthrew the Tsar.

...3

History of the end of Tsarism

Russian society in 1914

- Russia was a huge, backward country of 130 million people.
- Most Russians (90 per cent) were peasants in the countryside struggling to avoid starvation.
- Increasing numbers of Russians were moving to the towns to work in the factories, even though working and living conditions were terrible.
- A small group of Russians (1 per cent) were very rich. These were the landowners and new factory owners.

The government of Nicholas II in 1914

Government of Nicholas II up to the 1905 Revolution

- The Tsar had complete control of the government of Russia. He appointed the ministers to help him govern. He used the Okhrana (secret police) to remove any opposition.
- The Tsar was supported by the Orthodox Church. Its priests taught that it was a sin to oppose the Tsar.
- Despite poor living conditions and lack of political freedom, most Russians adored the Tsar and believed that their problems were caused by his ministers.

Opposition to the Tsar

- **Liberals** were educated, middle-class Russians who wanted an elected parliament to run Russia with the Tsar.
- **Social Revolutionaries** wanted the land to be divided among the peasants and taken from the great landowners. They also wanted to end the Tsar's rule.
- **Social Democrats** were communist. They too wanted to overthrow the Tsar, and set up a communist system in Russia. They appealed to the workers in the towns.

The powers of the Tsar meant that the leaders of revolutionary groups were in prison, in labour camps in Siberia or in exile abroad.

The 1905 Revolution

The 1905 Revolution had a great impact on Russia and has been called the 'dress rehearsal' for the 1917 Revolutions. Unfortunately for Nicholas II, he seemed to learn little from it.

- The 1905 Revolution was caused by bad harvests and discontent over Russia's defeats in the war with Japan.
- 'Bloody Sunday', January 1905. 200,000 workers led by Father Gapon marched to the Winter Palace to hand a petition to the Tsar. He was not there but his troops opened fire. Hundreds of marchers were killed.
- There was a strong reaction to Bloody Sunday, including strikes, attacks on property, and mutiny in the navy. Workers' soviets (councils) were set up to plan action.
- In October 1905, the Tsar backed down. In the October Manifesto he agreed to set up a Duma elected by the people. He also allowed freedom of speech.

Summary box 1

The 1905 Revolution
- Bad harvests
- Defeats in Russo–Japanese War
- Bloody Sunday
- Strikes, demonstrations and mutinies
- Workers' soviets
- October Manifesto and elected Duma

The period of the Dumas, 1906–14

- By 1906 the Tsar was in a stronger position. He issued the Fundamental Law giving him complete control over the Duma.
- There were four Dumas between 1906 and 1917. The first two Dumas were dismissed by Nicholas for asking for reforms. The last two survived longer because most of their members supported the Tsar.
- Opposition was crushed by the Okhrana. Revolutionaries were executed or sent to labour camps.
- Most leaders of the revolutionary groups were in exile, frightened to return to Russia. For example, Lenin was in Switzerland.

Summary box 2

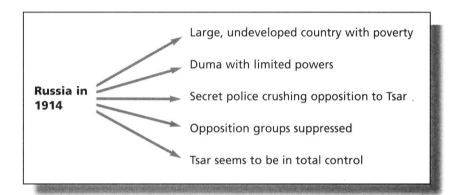

Russia in 1914
- Large, undeveloped country with poverty
- Duma with limited powers
- Secret police crushing opposition to Tsar .
- Opposition groups suppressed
- Tsar seems to be in total control

Impact of the First World War on Russia

When war was declared in 1914, there was great support for both the war and the Tsar. However, things soon began to change:

- Russian troops won some early victories but then lost at Tannenburg. The German army invaded Russia.
- The Russian armies were poorly equipped in weapons, uniforms and supplies. They were also badly led by weak generals.
- The war had a devastating effect on Russia. As well as the millions of soldiers killed, goods became expensive and there were shortages of food and raw materials such as coal. People were dying from starvation and cold.
- In 1915 the Tsar took personal control of the army and went to the front. This was unwise because:
  - He was now blamed for the Russian army's defeats.
  - Control of the government fell to his wife, the German-born Alexandra. She allowed the religious fanatic Rasputin to have a strong influence in the running of Russia. This made the Tsar's government more unpopular. Not even the assassination of Rasputin could end this growing unpopularity.

Summary box 3

The end of the Tsarist government: the March Revolution 1917

- The winter of 1916–17 was very cold and this made living conditions worse, with food and fuel shortages.
- In Petrograd there were strikes and demonstrations against the Tsar.
- On 11 March Nicholas ordered government troops to restore order in Petrograd.
- On 12 March the soldiers refused to fire on the demonstrators and instead began to join them. Petrograd was in the control of the revolutionaries.
- Members of the Duma set up a Provisional Government under Prince Lvov.
- Nicholas now decided to return to Petrograd. His train was stopped and his generals told him to give up the throne.
- Nicholas abdicated on 15 March.

The rule of the Tsars in Russia had come to an end.

Summary box 4

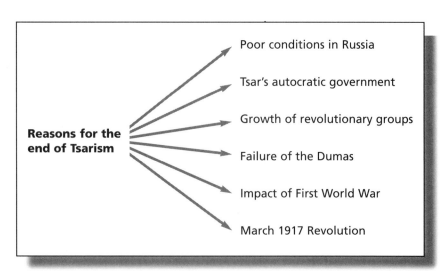

4

What do I Know?

What is the importance of the following:
- Bloody Sunday
- Rasputin?

1 What percentage of the Russian population in 1914 were peasants?
2 What was the name of the secret police force of the Tsar?
3 What did the Liberals want Russia to be like?
4 What did the Social Revolutionaries believe in?
5 When did Bloody Sunday take place?
6 What was a Duma?
7 Give one disadvantage of Nicholas II taking command of the army in 1915.
8 Who took over the government of Russia in March 1917?

My score ......

5

Exam Type Question

This is the kind of question found in Section A of Paper 2. It generally has one of the higher marks (10 marks) and so it is one of the more difficult questions you will face. It requires you to compare and evaluate two sources, using your knowledge to support your answer. The mark allocation is 7 marks for evaluating the sources and 3 marks for supporting knowledge. Look closely at the answers given and the examiner's comments on them.

Source A

▲ Photograph of Tsar Nicholas blessing Russian troops at the front in 1915.

Source B

> From the moment war broke out, it was obvious that the Russian forces were inferior to the Germans. Millions of men were drafted into the army but they were under the command of incompetent officers. The army was also poorly supplied. Desertion became common as morale fell.

▲ **From a book by a British historian, published in 1966.**

> Sources A and B give different interpretations of the First World War in Russia. Why do you think that these interpretations are different? Explain your answer using the sources and your own knowledge. **(10 marks)**

Answer 1

The two sources do offer different interpretations. Source A is a photograph taken at the time, showing the Tsar blessing his troops. It could be biased. It might have been taken to show how the army supported him. Source B is written by a British historian 50 years after the event. This is unlikely to be biased because the historian will have studied the subject before reaching any conclusions.

Answer 2

The two sources offer different interpretations but both are valid. Source A shows the Tsar blessing his troops. It is likely that this photograph has been set up and is biased to show how the Russian troops were ready to fight for the Tsar. However, it is true that at the start of the war there was great support for the Tsar. Also, when the Tsar took command of the army in 1915, he was supported by the troops. Source B is written after the event by an historian who will have studied the subject. From my knowledge, I know that the Russian army was very weak. There were shortages of weapons and food. The generals had little idea of modern fighting. The Russian army was easily defeated by the Germans. So the interpretations are different because they refer to different periods of the war.

Examiner's Comments: Answer 1

6 out of 10
The answer has its merits. It gives some detail to explain why the sources offer different interpretations. It touches on bias and motive. As such, it would receive 6 marks. It would not receive any higher mark because it has covered only one requirement of the question: it has evaluated the sources. However, there is no supporting knowledge and the second requirement has been omitted.

Answer 2

9 out of 10
You should easily see the difference in quality between this answer and Answer 1. Both have good evaluation of the sources. However, where Answer 1 does not move beyond this evaluation, Answer 2 has given supporting knowledge to explain the context of both sources – so it meets the second requirement of the question. This answer reaches the top level, 9 marks.

6

Practice Question

Now try to answer this question yourself.

Describe the effects of the First World War on Russia between 1914 and December 1916. **(5 marks)**

This is a short 'free standing' knowledge question – that is, it does not have a source to help or guide you. It is the kind of question that can be found in Section B of Paper 2. It requires you to provide a short, relevant answer that shows knowledge of the issue. After you have written your answer, look at Summary Box 3. Have you covered all the areas mentioned there?

4.2 The Provisional Government and the Bolshevik Revolution

1 Topic Summary

In March 1917, the Tsar had been overthrown. Russia was now ruled by the Provisional Government. When Russian defeats in the war continued, the Provisional Government became unpopular. People, especially in the towns, began to turn to Lenin and the Bolsheviks because they promised to end the war and to improve the conditions of the Russian people. In the revolution of November 1917 the Bolsheviks seized control of Petrograd and overthrew the Provisional Government.

2 What do I Need to Know?

You will need to understand why the Provisional Government became unpopular and failed to establish itself as the successor to the Tsar. You need to know that the Bolsheviks became popular because they offered different policies, especially in the promise to end the war. You will also need to know the reasons why the Bolsheviks seized control of Petrograd in November 1917 – their growing support and their organisation and planning.

> **The Russian calendar**
>
> Until 1918 Russia's calendar was thirteen days behind the Western calendar. This means that there are alternative dates for events depending on whether the old or the new calendar is used. So the first revolution of 1917 is the February or the March Revolution; and the Bolshevik Revolution of 1917 is the October or the November Revolution. In this book, we have used the Western calendar throughout.

3 History of the Provisional Government and the Bolshevik Revolution

The Provisional Government and its weaknesses

- The Provisional Government was made up of members of different political parties. This meant that they could not always agree on what to do.
- In Petrograd, real power lay with the Soviet (workers' council). This weakened the authority of the Provisional Government.
- The Provisional Government also faced the problem of what reforms to introduce. Many Russians wanted immediate changes. The government introduced some measures, such as freedom of speech, but these did not go far enough.
- The peasants wanted to own their land. The government decided to wait until a permanent government was elected.

- The Provisional Government decided to continue with the war. So all the problems of war which had existed under the Tsar – defeats, troops deserting, food and fuel shortages – continued. This was the most unpopular decision of the Provisional Government.
- After the March Revolution many of the revolutionary leaders began to return to Russia. They now criticised the Provisional Government. Most important among these was Lenin, leader of the Bolsheviks.

Summary box 1

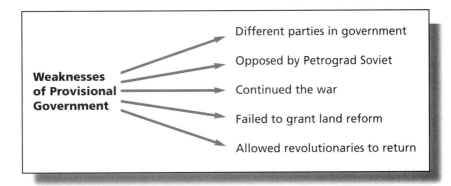

Weaknesses of Provisional Government
- Different parties in government
- Opposed by Petrograd Soviet
- Continued the war
- Failed to grant land reform
- Allowed revolutionaries to return

The Bolsheviks, April to September 1917

- In April, Lenin, helped by the Germans, returned to Russia.
- Lenin issued the 'April Theses' promising 'Peace, Bread and Land' to the people.
- The July Days. In July, the Provisional Government ordered an attack on Germany which ended in Russian defeat. When news of this defeat reached Petrograd, soldiers, sailors and workers demonstrated against the Provisional Government. The Bolsheviks joined the demonstrators and rioting broke out. Troops loyal to the government put down the rising. Lenin was forced to flee from Russia and Bolshevik leaders were arrested.
- In September, General Kornilov tried to seize power. The Bolsheviks helped to defeat him – and kept the weapons given to them by the government.
- By September the Bolsheviks had control of the Petrograd and Moscow Soviets.

The November Revolution and the Bolshevik seizure of power

November Revolution

- During the autumn, Trotsky prepared a detailed plan for revolution. It aimed to overthrow the Provisional Government by seizing control of Petrograd.
- When Lenin returned to Russia in October, the decision was made to carry out the plan. It was put into operation on 7–8 November.

- The key to the plan was to capture all the important buildings in Petrograd as quickly as possible, e.g. the State Bank and the Telephone Exchange; this would be done by the Red Guards.
- The Bolsheviks also had the support of a cruiser, the *Aurora*.
- The Provisional Government had little support and its members were trapped in the Winter Palace.
- Kerensky, the leader of the Provisional Government, fled from Petrograd.
- The Winter Palace was stormed by the Red Guards and the Provisional Government surrendered.
- Lenin proclaimed a new government for Russia.

The Bolsheviks now had to extend their control to the rest of Russia.

Summary box 2

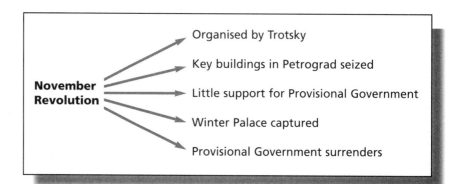

November Revolution
- Organised by Trotsky
- Key buildings in Petrograd seized
- Little support for Provisional Government
- Winter Palace captured
- Provisional Government surrenders

Summary box 3

Reasons for Bolshevik success
- Weakness of the Provisional Government
- Unpopularity of the Provisional Government
- Continuation of the war
- Promises of Lenin and the Bolsheviks
- Organisation of the Bolsheviks
- Seizure of Petrograd

Key Dates To Learn

1914		Russia enters the First World War
1917	**March**	Nicholas II overthrown by revolution
		Provisional Government set up
	April	Lenin returns to Russia; 'April Theses'
	July	'July Days' – attempted revolution fails
	September	Kornilov Affair
	November	Bolsheviks seize control of Petrograd
		Provisional Government overthrown

...4

What do I Know?

1 Give one reason why the Provisional Government was unpopular with the people.
2 Who helped Lenin to return to Russia in 1917?
3 What slogan did the Bolsheviks have?
4 What were the 'July Days'?
5 Which army commander tried to take control of Russia in September 1917?
6 Name two kinds of buildings seized by the Bolsheviks in the revolution of 1917.
7 Which building was stormed by the Bolsheviks in the revolution?

My score ......

What is the importance of the following:
- The April Theses
- November Revolution 1917?

...5

Exam Type Question

This is the kind of question that can be found in Section A of Paper 2. It generally has a value of 5 marks. Remember the following:

1 It requires you to examine a source and draw conclusions from that source.

2 No additional knowledge is needed and your answer should cover only what is in the source.

3 Whatever the kind of source, there will always be plenty of information to allow you to make some comment.

Look closely at the answers given and the examiner's comments on them.

> No resistance was shown to the Bolsheviks in Petrograd. Beginning at 2am, the railway stations, bridges, electricity plants and telegraphs were occupied by the Red Guards. These operations were bloodless; not one casualty was reported. The city was absolutely calm.

▲ From N Sukhanov, an eyewitness during the November Revolution, 1917.

Explain what you can learn from the source about the reasons why the Bolsheviks took control of Petrograd in the revolution of November 1917. **(5 marks)**

Answer 1

The source shows that the Bolsheviks quickly took control of Petrograd during the night. This is because no one opposed them.

Answer 2

The source shows that the Bolsheviks were well organised. They took control of the important buildings in Petrograd like the stations and electricity plants. They were also helped by the fact that no one resisted them - the city was calm. This could be because the revolution was supported by the people of Petrograd or that they were taken by surprise.

Examiner's Comments: Answer 1

2 out of 5

This is a short answer but it does have some merit. It indicates that the revolution was successful and that the main reason for this is the fact that there was no opposition to the Bolsheviks. So there is a basic understanding and a conclusion is reached.

Answer 2

5 out of 5

A much stronger answer. It picks out the two main reasons given in the source to explain why the Bolsheviks were successful – their organisation and the lack of resistance to them. It also gives examples from the source to support these conclusions. The final sentence concludes the answer and shows that the candidate has given the source a little extra thought.

Practice Question

Now try to answer this question yourself.

Describe the weaknesses of the Provisional Government in Russia.

(5 marks)

This is a short 'free-standing' knowledge question – that is, it does not have a source to help or guide you. It is the kind of question that can be found in Section B of Paper 2. It generally has a value of 5 marks. Remember the following:

1 It requires you to produce a short, relevant answer that shows knowledge of the issue.

2 It is relatively easy – provided you have revised.

4.3 The creation of a Communist State, 1917–24

1 Topic Summary

In the November Revolution, the Bolsheviks had taken control of Petrograd. They now extended their control to the rest of Russia. Some early actions were popular – the war ended and land was given to the people. However, a communist dictatorship was soon set up: Russia became a 'totalitarian' state. Opposition to the communists led to a bitter civil war, and the anti-communist 'Whites' were defeated. Conditions in Russia remained poor, and the increase of state control during War Communism only made things worse. Lenin then changed to a New Economic Policy (NEP) with less state control. Despite all these problems, by Lenin's death in 1924, the communists were firmly in power.

2 What do I Need to Know?

You will need to understand how Lenin and the Bolsheviks imposed their control over Russia – partly by keeping their promises of 'land and peace' and partly by removing all opposition. The Civil War is an important area of study because it confirmed communist control. You will need to know why civil war broke out and the reasons why the Reds were able to defeat the Whites. Finally, you should understand the two economic policies of this period: War Communism and NEP, and note their similarities and their differences.

In Section 4.2 we talked about the Bolsheviks. During 1918 the Bolsheviks changed their name to the communists. So for the remainder of your study of Russia you should refer to the party of Lenin and Stalin as the Communist Party.

3 History of the creation of a Communist State

Establishment of communist control in Russia

After November 1917 the Bolsheviks tried to extend their control over the rest of Russia. Some of the policies they introduced were popular:

- A land decree took land away from the landowners and the Orthodox Church, and gave it to the peasants.
- Working hours in factories were limited to a maximum of eight hours a day.
- Peace was made. The Treaty of Brest-Litovsk in 1918 took Russia out of the First World War, but at a huge cost: Russia lost one-quarter of its land and half of its industry. Lenin felt that he had to accept these terms if communist rule was to survive.

Some of the actions of the communists were harsh. A communist dictatorship was set up:

- Elections were held for a Constituent Assembly – a parliament. When the communists did not win enough seats to form a government, Lenin abolished the Assembly.
- A new secret police, the Cheka, was used to crush opposition. In 1918 it began a Red Terror in which thousands of Russians were executed or placed in concentration camps.

Summary box 1

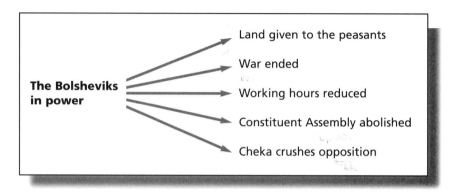

The Bolsheviks in power

- Land given to the peasants
- War ended
- Working hours reduced
- Constituent Assembly abolished
- Cheka crushes opposition

The Civil War in Russia, 1918–21

Causes of the Civil War

The Bolsheviks had taken their opponents by surprise when they seized control of Petrograd. In 1918 the opposition joined together as the 'Whites' to try to defeat the 'Reds'. The Whites consisted of:

- Supporters of the Tsar, including most army officers.
- Landowners who had lost their land.
- Supporters of the Provisional Government.

The Whites were helped by armies sent by foreign powers such as Britain and the USA who opposed communism and were annoyed when Russia withdrew from the war.

Reasons for the communist success in the Civil War

- The Whites were disunited, coming from different groups with nothing in common apart from hatred of the communists.
- The armies of the Whites were poorly led and did not co-operate with each other.
- The Red Army was well organised by Trotsky. He built up an army of volunteers and conscripts, and controlled it with strong discipline.
- The Reds controlled the railway network so troops could be moved around easily.
- The Russian people were more favourable to the communists who had given them land. Also, the use of foreign armies by the Whites was unpopular.

Results of the Civil War

- There was great violence from both sides. A famine in 1921 made things even worse.
- The war confirmed the communist victory in Russia.
- The war brought the end of Tsarism. In July 1918, Nicholas II and his family were executed by Red forces, in case the Whites rescued them.

Summary box 2

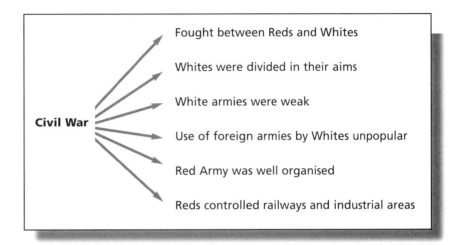

Civil War
- Fought between Reds and Whites
- Whites were divided in their aims
- White armies were weak
- Use of foreign armies by Whites unpopular
- Red Army was well organised
- Reds controlled railways and industrial areas

Economic policy

War Communism

This was the economic policy during the Civil War. Its aim was to make sure that the Red Army was well supplied with weapons and food.

- The state took control of all factories.
- Food was rationed.
- Grain was taken from the peasants without payment. This led to food shortages because peasants preferred to grow less rather than give it away.

New Economic Policy

War Communism brought unrest in Russia. This was seen in 1921 when sailors at Kronstadt revolted. Lenin realised that his economic policy had to change – especially as the Civil War was now over.

- Small businesses were returned to private ownership.
- Peasants were allowed to sell their surplus grain for profit.
- Many communists saw the NEP as a betrayal of their ideas because farmers and traders (NEPmen) became rich on the profits of trade.
- However, all the important sections of the economy stayed under state control.

Summary box 3

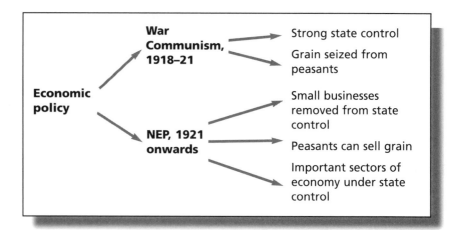

Creation of the USSR

- By 1923 Russia became the Union of Soviet Socialist Republics (USSR). At first there were four republics, the largest of which was Russia.
- Lenin died in January 1924. His achievement was to bring the communists to power in the November Revolution and then to make sure that communist rule survived.

Key Dates To Learn

1917	November Revolution and Bolshevik victory
1918	Red Terror against opposition
	Treaty of Brest-Litovsk takes Russia out of First World War
	Assassination of Nicholas II and the royal family
1918–21	Civil War
	War Communism
1921	Kronstadt Revolt
	New Economic Policy
1923	Russia becomes the USSR
1924	Death of Lenin

4

What do I Know?

What is the importance of the following:
- The Civil War
- War Communism
- NEP?

1 What was the Cheka?
2 Which treaty took Russia out of the First World War?
3 How was this treaty harsh on Russia?
4 Who organised the Red Army in the Civil War?
5 What different groups formed the Whites in the Civil War?
6 Give one difference between War Communism and the NEP.
7 Where was there a naval mutiny against the Bolsheviks in 1921?
8 What new name was given to Russia in 1923?

My score ......

5

Exam Type Question

This is the kind of question that can be found in Section B of Paper 2. It generally carries 7 marks. It requires you to do two things:

1 Use the evidence in the source to answer the question.

2 Use your knowledge to explain your answer. This can be done by giving further information on the source. You should then go on to give additional information from your own knowledge.

Look closely at the answer given and the examiner's comments. Then answer the practice question.

Output (in millions of tons)		
	1913	**1921**
Coal	29.0	9.0
Oil	9.2	3.8
Iron	4.2	0.1
Steel	4.3	0.2
Grain	80.0	37.6

◀ **Production in the USSR: a comparison between 1913 and 1921.**

Use the source and your own knowledge to explain why Lenin replaced War Communism with the NEP in 1921. **(7 marks)**

Answer

The source shows that War Communism was not working. Grain production had fallen from 80 million tons to 37.6 million tons. All the industries had falling output – coal, oil, iron and steel. Lenin realised that changes had to be made so he introduced the NEP.

Examiner's Comments

2 out of 7

This is a limited answer. It is based completely on the evidence in the source. There is no additional or supporting knowledge. So, only one of the two requirements of the question has been met and, as this is the less important requirement in terms of the marks allocated to it, the answer suffers.

6

Practice Question

Now try to answer the question above yourself.

The mark allocation for this type of question is 5 marks for knowledge and 2 marks for using the evidence in the source. You must make sure that your answer reflects this mark allocation.

4.4 The rule of Stalin, 1924–41

1

Topic Summary

After Lenin's death, there was a struggle for power between Trotsky and Stalin before Stalin emerged as the new leader of the USSR. He set up a personal dictatorship, removing all rivals from power and purging (eliminating) any group that might oppose him. His control was strengthened by the use of censorship and propaganda.

Stalin wanted to make the USSR a great economic power and used ruthless methods to achieve this. Industry was reorganised in the Five-Year Plans, and agriculture was brought under state control by collectivisation. These changes brought great suffering to the Russian people – but they also allowed the USSR to survive the Second World War.

2

What do I Need to Know?

You will need to understand why Stalin, rather than Trotsky, became leader of the Communist Party and the USSR. You need to know how Stalin used purges to remove opposition and how he strengthened his control of the USSR by propaganda and censorship (the 'cult of personality') and by terror. The other topic in this section is economic policy: you need to understand the changes Stalin made to industry and agriculture, and how successful these changes were.

3

History of the rule of Stalin

Stalin's dictatorship

The struggle for power with Trotsky

- When Lenin died in 1924, a successor had not been appointed. However, the favourite was Trotsky who had been Lenin's closest associate. Lenin had regarded Stalin as unsuitable.
- Stalin's policy of 'socialism in one country' was more popular than Trotsky's idea of a worldwide 'permanent revolution'.
- Stalin was General Secretary of the Communist Party. This meant that he could appoint supporters to positions in the Party.
- In 1925 Trotsky was removed as Commissar (Minister) for War. In 1929 Stalin exiled him from the USSR.
- Between 1926 and 1929 Stalin removed other possible rivals from the Communist Party.
- In this way, Stalin gained full control of the Communist Party and of the USSR.

The purges and the Great Terror

Although Stalin was in control of the USSR by the end of the 1920s, he never felt completely secure. So he removed opponents by purges and frightened ordinary Russians by his use of terror:

- Those who opposed him or his policies were arrested and sent to labour camps.
- Leading communists were purged in 'show trials', the most famous being Kamenev and Zinoviev, who confessed that they were in league with Trotsky and had been plotting against Stalin. During the show trials Stalin's rivals were forced to confess to crimes, which gave Stalin the excuse to get rid of them.
- Army officers were also purged; many were executed.
- Millions of ordinary Russians were arrested in the Great Terror. They were reported to the NKVD (secret police) by neighbours, fellow workers and friends.
- Most of Stalin's victims were classed as 'enemies of the state'. Over 20 million people were sent to labour camps in remote areas such as Siberia. A large proportion never returned.

Propaganda and censorship: the cult of personality

- Propaganda was used to show how great a leader Stalin was.
- Newspapers were controlled by the Communist Party.
- Censorship was used to glorify Stalin and the communist revolution. Paintings, posters, films, books and music were all controlled.
- History books were rewritten to show Stalin's importance in the communist revolution. All references to Trotsky were removed.

Constitution of 1936

- This confirmed the control of the Communist Party over the USSR. By doing so it also confirmed Stalin's control over the USSR.
- Although the USSR looked like a democracy, with elections to a parliament, the Communist Party was the only legal political party.

Summary box 1

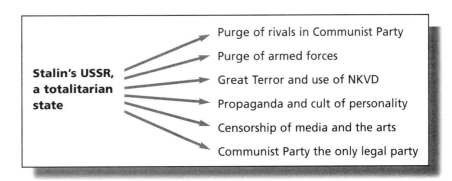

Stalin's USSR, a totalitarian state
- Purge of rivals in Communist Party
- Purge of armed forces
- Great Terror and use of NKVD
- Propaganda and cult of personality
- Censorship of media and the arts
- Communist Party the only legal party

Stalin's economic policy

The Russian economy had suffered because of war, revolution and civil war. Stalin was determined to make the economy strong. He believed that, if this was not done, the USSR might not survive. For Stalin, both agriculture and industry needed to be improved as quickly as possible.

Agriculture

Stalin had two aims for agriculture:

- Improve food production, to feed the new industrial workers and to export food abroad to buy foreign machinery.
- Remove the kulaks – rich peasants who, Stalin claimed, were opposed to communism.

Collectivisation

- Peasants' land was collectivised (grouped together) to form large farms called *kolkhoz*.
- The state set targets for food production for each collective farm.
- Tractors and other machinery were placed on the farms to help production.
- At first all land was taken from the peasants. This was unpopular so they were allowed to keep small plots around their cottages.
- Peasants who refused to join the collective farms (mostly kulaks) were arrested and sent to labour camps

Results of collectivisation

- Food production fell between 1929 and 1933 because peasants often destroyed their crops and slaughtered their animals in protest against collectivisation.
- Over 13 million peasants died during the 1930s – from starvation and because they opposed collectivisation.

However,

- From 1933, food production began to rise.
- By 1937, 90 per cent of Russian farms were collectivised.

Summary box 2

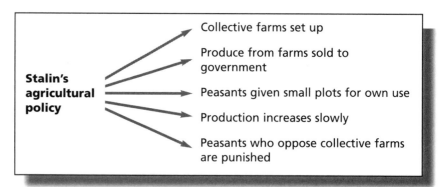

Industry

Five-Year Plans

- Stalin believed in strong state control and planning to improve industrial production.
- Gosplan (the state planning agency) set targets for growth in industrial production in a series of Five-Year Plans.

- There were three Five-Year Plans, beginning in 1928, 1933 and 1938. Although there were differences between them, all concentrated on heavy industry.

Results of the Five-Year Plans

- Production increased greatly in coal, iron, steel and oil.
- New towns, steel plants, coalmines and dams were built. Many were located in 'safe' areas, away from possible invasion.
- By 1939, the USSR had become one of the world's great industrial powers.

However, the cost to the Russian people was immense:

- Forced labour was used to build factories, railways and canals.
- Living and working conditions in towns were terrible. Food shortages meant that rationing was common.
- Workers who did not reach their targets were punished – often by sentence to gulags (labour camps).
- Few consumer goods were produced to improve the quality of life.

Summary box 3

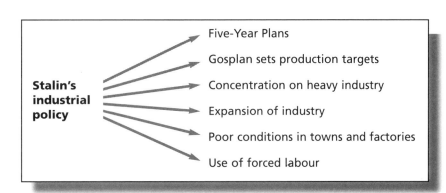

Stalin's industrial policy
- Five-Year Plans
- Gosplan sets production targets
- Concentration on heavy industry
- Expansion of industry
- Poor conditions in towns and factories
- Use of forced labour

4

What do I Know?

1 Who was Stalin's great rival for power in 1924?
2 What were the 'show trials'?
3 What kinds of things were censored during Stalin's rule?
4 What was the 'cult of personality'?
5 What was Gosplan?
6 How many Five-Year Plans were there?
7 Give one feature of a collective farm.
8 Which groups of peasants suffered most in collectivisation?

My score ......

What is the importance of the following:
- Purges
- Collectivisation
- Five-Year Plans?

5

.........5..

Exam Type Question

This is a short 'essay' or extended writing question and can be the hardest part of the exam. On Paper 2 you have to answer two questions of this type – one in Section A and one in Section B. Together they account for 30 of the 75 marks on Paper 2, so it is important that you answer them well. Look closely at the answer given and the examiner's comments on it.

> Explain how Stalin took personal control of the USSR in the years 1924 to 1939. **(15 marks)**

Answer

Once Lenin had died, Stalin quickly became the dictator of Russia. He did this in a number of ways.

He introduced purges to get rid of opponents or anyone he thought was an opponent. Rivals in the Communist Party were purged. Trotsky, his greatest rival, was exiled from Russia. Others were put on show trials where they confessed to all kinds of crimes. The verdict was always guilty and they were executed. The officers in the army and navy were also purged because Stalin did not trust them. Ordinary Russians also suffered. A Great Terror organised by the secret police sent millions of Russians to labour camps or to execution.

Stalin also achieved control by the use of propaganda. All newspapers and books were censored so that only good things about Stalin were written. Paintings, posters and films were used to glorify Stalin and show how great he was. This was called the cult of personality and it made Stalin seem like a god.

So in these ways, terror and propaganda, Stalin was able to take personal control of the USSR.

Examiner's Comments

12 out of 15

This is a strong answer showing plenty of knowledge. It covers the show trials of communist rivals, the purges of the armed forces and the Great Terror. It also mentions censorship and propaganda, covering a range of examples and showing how this links into the cult of personality. However, although mention is made of the exile of Trotsky, there is no coverage of how Stalin managed to defeat him. Perhaps the importance of the date 1924 as the beginning of the question was not realised. This is why you should be aware of important dates in your revision.

6

Practice Question

Now try to answer this sort of question yourself.

Was Stalin's collectivisation policy for Russian agriculture a success? Explain your answer. **(15 marks)**

Some guidelines on answering the question are:

1 Answer the question set. You do not have time to give information that is not relevant and you will not be rewarded for doing so.

2 Always try to back up a statement with some knowledge.

3 Try to write a detailed answer. You should have at least 20 minutes to answer the question.

5 Germany, 1918–39

5.1 The Weimar Republic, 1918–33

Topic Summary

In November 1918 the armistice ended the war. The Kaiser abdicated and a German Republic – the Weimar Republic – was proclaimed. It was blamed for signing the Treaty of Versailles and all the problems that resulted from it. These early problems were solved and after 1923 it looked as if the Weimar Republic would bring wealth and stability to Germany. However, it failed to deal with the Depression of 1929 and, as conditions grew worse, the German people turned to more extreme parties. By 1933 the Nazi Party had taken control and the Weimar Republic had ended.

What do I Need to Know?

You will need to know the problems facing the Weimar Republic in 1919 and how these problems worsened up to 1923. You will also need to understand the problems created by hyperinflation in the economic crisis of 1923. Despite these problems, you should realise that the Republic did survive and that Germany was prosperous between 1924 and 1929. Finally, you will need to know how the Depression came to Germany in 1929 and how failure to deal with it brought the Weimar Republic to an end.

History of the Weimar Republic

Early problems of the Weimar Republic

Reaction to the Treaty of Versailles

- The Treaty was hated by the German people and they blamed the politicians of the Republic for signing it. They thought the politicians had 'stabbed the army in the back'.
- Germans resented the fact that Germany had to accept blame for the war (the 'War Guilt' clause) and that the Treaty was forced on them. They were made to pay reparations; the sum was fixed at £6600 million in 1921.
- Germans resented the harsh terms imposed at Versailles: Germany lost a large amount of territory, and its military power was severely cut back.

Political challenges

There were left-wing uprisings that tried to overthrow the Republic:

- Berlin (1919). The Spartacists (communists) were defeated by the army.
- Bavaria (1919). A socialist republic was set up, but government troops defeated it.

There were right-wing rebellions against the Republic:

- Berlin (1920). The Kapp *Putsch* (uprising), led by Wolfgang Kapp, was defeated by a general strike organised by the workers.
- Munich (1923). A Nazi *Putsch* was defeated by the authorities.

Weimar constitution

Despite being democratic, the constitution of the Weimar Republic brought problems:

- A voting system of proportional representation meant that small parties gained seats in the Reichstag. No one party had a majority and so coalition governments of a number of different parties had to be formed. These coalitions were weak because they could not get agreement on policies.
- The system allowed extreme parties like the Nazis and communists to gain seats in the Reichstag.

Summary box 1

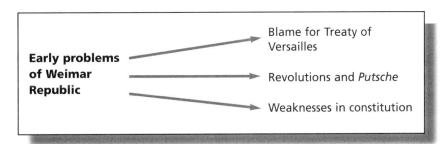

Economic problems, 1923

- In 1921 the German government was ordered to pay £6600 million to the Allies as reparations for the war. In 1922 the government announced that Germany could not afford the payments. The French then invaded the Ruhr, Germany's main industrial area, to take by force what they were owed. But workers there went on strike as part of passive resistance to the French invasion and industrial production ground to a halt.
- The government tried to solve the problem by printing more money. Money lost its value and prices went out of control. For example, in 1918 a loaf of bread cost 0.6 marks; in January 1923 it cost 250 marks; in November 1923 it cost 201,000 million marks. This is called hyperinflation.

Winners from hyperinflation

- Borrowers. Money borrowed in 1919 was now worthless and could easily be paid back.
- Big business. Exporters could sell goods abroad in exchange for more valuable currencies.
- Landowners. As prices went up so did the value of land.

Losers from hyperinflation

- Workers. The price of goods always rose faster than wages.
- Savers. Those with life savings in the bank found that their money was worthless.
- People on fixed incomes, like pensioners. Their incomes were now too low to live on.
- Small businesses. They could not deal with the rapid changes in prices.

Summary box 2

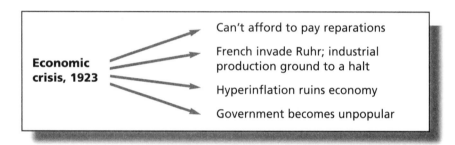

Economic crisis, 1923 →
- Can't afford to pay reparations
- French invade Ruhr; industrial production ground to a halt
- Hyperinflation ruins economy
- Government becomes unpopular

Recovery of Weimar Republic, 1924–29

Gustav Stresemann became the leading politician in Germany in 1923. He brought in measures which restored the German economy and improved relations with other countries. This period is sometimes called 'the golden age of the Weimar Republic'. Stresemann died in 1929, just as the Depression hit Germany.

Economic recovery under Stresemann

- Hyperinflation was solved by the introduction of a new currency, the Rentenmark.
- In 1924 the Dawes Plan allowed Germany to pay reparations according to its ability to do so. It also arranged loans from the USA.
- The French left the Ruhr once reparation payments were resumed.
- The Young Plan of 1929 gave Germany a further 59 years to pay reparations.

International relations

Relations with other countries were improved by the signing of the Locarno Treaty in 1925 and the Kellogg-Briand Pact in 1928. Germany was invited to join the League of Nations in 1926. It meant that Germany was again accepted by the other powers.

However, many Germans were concerned that prosperity was based on loans from abroad, especially from the USA.

Summary box 3

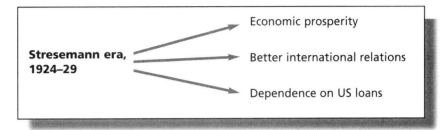

Stresemann era, 1924–29
→ Economic prosperity
→ Better international relations
→ Dependence on US loans

The Depression, 1929–33

- In 1929 the Wall Street Crash forced US banks to recall their loans to Germany.
- German industry was hit by a fall in demand and was unable to pay back loans from the USA.
- Millions of workers were made unemployed as factories closed down.
- None of the measures introduced by the government to combat the Depression had any effect, which brought out all the weaknesses of the Weimar Republic.
- Coalition groups were formed as different parties disagreed on how to end the Depression, but it proved impossible to form a coalition government.
- After 1929 a political emergency was declared and Germany was ruled by the emergency powers of the President.
- Extreme parties like the Nazis and the communists won increased support because they promised to do something to end the Depression.
- In 1933 the Weimar government was replaced by a Nazi dictatorship.

Key Dates To Learn

1918	End of war; abdication of Kaiser William
	New republic set up
1919	Spartacist uprising
	Weimar constitution set up
	Treaty of Versailles signed
1920	Kapp *Putsch*
1923	French occupation of the Ruhr
	Hyperinflation crisis
	Munich *Putsch*
1924	Dawes Plan
1925	Germany signs Locarno Pact
	French leave the Ruhr
1926	Germany joins League of Nations
1929	Wall Street Crash and Depression in Germany
	Death of Stresemann

4 What do I Know?

What is the importance of the following:

- Proportional representation in Weimar Germany
- Hyperinflation?

1 What was the 'War Guilt' clause of the Treaty of Versailles?

2 Who did the German people think had 'stabbed them in the back'?

3 Who were the Spartacists?

4 What did Kapp do?

5 What is a *Putsch*?

6 What was the name of the plan of 1924 by which the USA lent Germany money?

7 How did the Wall Street Crash bring Depression to Germany in 1929?

My score ......

5 Exam Type Question

Here is the sort of essay question you might be asked in Paper 2 of the exam paper. Look closely at the answer given and the examiner's comments.

Explain how the Treaty of Versailles created problems for Germany in the period 1919 to 1924. **(15 marks)**

Answer

The Treaty of Versailles was signed in 1919. It was hated by the German people and was one of the reasons why Hitler came to power.

The Treaty of Versailles took a lot of land from Germany and gave it to other countries like France, Poland, Denmark and Belgium. Some of this land was valuable. Alsace-Lorraine had coal and iron and its loss weakened Germany. Germany was also divided by the Polish Corridor. The Germans in East Prussia were now separated from Germany.

The Treaty also weakened Germany's military power. The army was limited to 100,000 men and there were even stronger restrictions on the air force and navy. The area bordering France - the Rhineland - was demilitarised and no German troops were allowed there. This meant that Germany could not defend itself. The fall in the size of the army also brought unemployment.

The Treaty placed reparations on Germany. Germany had to pay for the war. Before long Germany said that it couldn't pay the huge amount. So in 1923 the French invaded the Ruhr to seize the coal there. The German government printed more money to pay the reparations but all this did was to make money worthless. Germany suffered from hyperinflation as prices shot up. People with savings were ruined.

The Treaty of Versailles was very harsh on Germany and caused a lot of problems. It weakened the Weimar Republic.

Examiner's Comments

13 out of 15

There is much in the answer that is very positive. The candidate clearly knows a lot about the details of the Treaty of Versailles. More importantly, the candidate also understands how this affected Germany through loss of land, disarmament and reparations. The one area with weaknesses is the effect on the German people of war guilt and the dictated peace. There might also have been some reference to the recovery of Germany after 1924. Overall this is a strong answer that would reach the top level.

6

Practice Question

Now try to answer this sort of question yourself.

Explain why there was so much opposition to the Weimar Republic between 1919 and 1924. **(15 marks)**

This is a short 'essay' or extended writing question and can be the hardest part of the exam. On Paper 2 you have to answer two questions of this type – one in Section A and one in Section B. Together they account for 30 of the 75 marks on this paper so it is important that you answer them well. The question requires you to use your knowledge. Some general guidelines are:

1 Answer the question set. You have not the time to give information that is not relevant, nor will you be rewarded for it.
2 Always try to back up a statement with some knowledge.
3 Look to write a detailed answer. You should have at least 20 minutes to answer the question.

5.2 Hitler and the growth of the Nazi Party to 1933

1 Topic Summary

The Nazi Party was a right-wing party formed in 1920. It was small and at first had little success. An attempted *Putsch* in Munich in 1923 failed and Hitler was arrested. During the years of prosperity (1924–29) the Nazi Party remained small. In the Depression, the German people became attracted to the ideas of the Nazis, laid down in *Mein Kampf*, and to the promise to end Germany's economic problems. The Nazis became the biggest party in the Reichstag in July 1932. In January 1933, Hitler was appointed Chancellor.

2 What do I Need to Know?

You will need to know about the early years of the Nazi Party – from its foundation in 1920 to the failure of the Munich *Putsch* in 1923. It is important to understand the main ideas of the Nazi Party and to see how they would be attractive to the German people. The Nazi Party remained small from 1924 to 1929 but you should be aware of how it developed in that period. Finally, you need to understand how Depression brought increased support to the Nazis and allowed them, and Hitler, to come to power.

3 History of Hitler and the Nazi Party's rise to power

Early years, 1920–2

- Hitler joined the German Workers' Party in 1919 as the seventh member.
- This became the National Socialist German Workers Party (Nazi Party) in 1920, with Hitler as leader.
- The Stormtroopers (SA) were set up in 1921. They were a private army used to 'protect' Nazi meetings and to attack opponents of the Nazis.

Nazi beliefs

These were stated in the Nazi Party programme of 1920 and further developed by Hitler in *Mein Kampf* in 1924.

- **Race.** The Aryan race, which included the German people, was a master race. Other races were inferior and should be removed.
- ***Lebensraum.*** Germans were entitled to 'living space' in Eastern Europe and should take control of countries like Poland.
- The Treaty of Versailles must be destroyed and Germany's possessions and people returned to it.
- **One leader.** Hitler believed in a strong leader with total control of a united empire (*Reich*).
- **Strength.** Hitler believed in a strong army to make Germany great again.

- **Anti-Semitism.** Jews were used as scapegoats and blamed for weakening Germany and for Germany's defeat in the First World War.
- **Anti-communism.** Hitler believed that communists were also weakening Germany.

Munich Putsch, 1923

The Weimar Republic's economic problems made it unpopular. Hitler thought that the time was right to try to overthrow it.

- 8 November. Hitler and 600 Stormtroopers entered a beer hall in Munich. Hitler declared himself President of Germany.
- 9 November. Hitler and his supporters marched on Munich.
- The state police and army remained loyal to the government. Hitler had overestimated the support he would receive and he was arrested.
- At his trial Hitler made speeches against all the groups he opposed and against the Weimar Republic. The trial made him a hero to many Germans.
- Hitler was sentenced to five years' imprisonment but served only nine months. During this time Hitler wrote *Mein Kampf,* outlining many of the views which he later put into practice.

Summary box 1

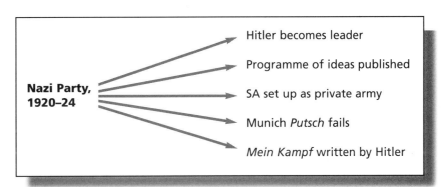

The Nazi Party, 1924–29

- As the German economy improved, the Nazi Party made little progress. It held only twelve seats in the Reichstag in 1925.
- However, the number of members tripled in this period, helped by rallies and public meetings across Germany. Membership increased from 27,000 in 1925 to over 100,00 in 1928.
- Support for the Nazis grew, especially among certain groups of Germans who were attracted by Nazi ideas. These were:
  - Nationalists who wanted to destroy the Treaty of Versailles.
  - Racists who hated the Jews and believed that Germans were superior.
  - Businesspeople who feared communism.
  - Young people attracted by the parades and the future hope of a 'great Germany'.

Growth of support for the Nazi Party, 1929–33

Effects of the Depression

- The Weimar Republic could not solve the problems of the Depression (see Section 5.1).
- The Nazis promised to end the Depression and unemployment.
- The Nazis were well organised and used propaganda to put over their message via posters, rallies and meetings. The SA also disrupted opponents' meetings.

Electoral gains

- 1930 Reichstag election: Nazis won 107 seats.
- July 1932 Reichstag election: Nazis won 230 seats and became the largest party.
- November 1932 Reichstag election: Nazis won 196 seats and remained the largest party.
- April 1932 Presidential election: Hitler lost to Hindenburg but 13 million Germans voted for him.

Hitler becomes Chancellor, January 1933

Despite his dislike of Hitler, the strength of the Nazis in the Reichstag forced President Hindenburg to accept Hitler as Chancellor. Three other Nazis also entered the government. Hindenburg and other politicians, like the Vice-Chancellor, Von Papen, still expected that they could control Hitler.

Key Dates To Learn

1919	Hitler joins the German Workers' Party	
1920	Hitler becomes leader and renames it the Nazi Party	
1921	SA set up	
1923	Hitler fails to take power in the Munich *Putsch*	
1924	Hitler imprisoned; writes *Mein Kampf*	
1928	Nazi Party wins 12 seats in the Reichstag	
1929	Depression hits Germany	
1930	Nazis win 107 seats in the Reichstag	
1932	**April**	Hitler wins 13 million votes in election for President
	July	Nazis win 230 seats in the Reichstag
	November	Nazis win 196 seats in the Reichstag
1933	**January**	Hitler appointed Chancellor

...4

What do I Know?

What is the importance of the following:

- *Mein Kampf*
- the Depression in Germany, 1930–33?

1 What was the 'Aryan race'?

2 What was meant by *Lebensraum*?

3 Name two groups that supported the Nazis.

4 Who were the SA?

5 What does 'anti-Semitism' mean?

6 What did the Nazis promise the German people in the 1932 election?

7 Who invited Hitler to become Chancellor in 1933?

8 Why was Hitler not in complete control when he was made Chancellor?

My score ......

...5

Exam Type Question

Here is the sort of source-based question you might be asked in Section A of Paper 2. Look closely at the answers given and the examiner's comments on them. Then answer the practice question.

▼ 1932 Nazi election posters.

Source B

'Women! Millions of men out of work! Millions of children without a future! Vote for Adolf Hitler!'

Source A

'We want work and bread. Elect Hitler!'

Look at Sources A and B. Do they agree about the message put forward by the Nazis in the 1932 Reichstag election? **(6 marks)**

Answer

The sources agree. Source A says that people should vote for Hitler because they want work. Source B says that people should vote for Hitler because millions of men are out of work.

Examiner's Comments

2 out of 6

This kind of answer must be avoided! All it does is describe the sources and it does not explain them. To get full marks the candidate would need to explain the ways in which the posters are similar and also the different appeal of the two posters.

6

Practice Question

Now have a go at the above question yourself. When answering the question, remember the following:

1 It requires you to look at two sources and compare them – that is, to explain the ways in which they are similar and the ways in which they are different.
2 You are not awarded marks for knowledge in this question so make sure that you use the sources only.

5.3 Establishment of a Nazi Dictatorship, 1933–34

...*1*

Topic Summary

After Hitler became Chancellor, he set about establishing a dictatorship. This was achieved between January 1933 and August 1934 when he removed all opposition to the Nazi Party. He even destroyed the SA because he thought they were becoming a threat to him within the Party. Nazi ministers and officials were appointed to allow Hitler to control all aspects of government in Germany. Finally, the death of President Hindenburg gave Hitler total control and he became Führer.

...*2*

What do I Need to Know?

This is a relatively short period of time but there are a number of key events that allowed Hitler to gain total power. You will need to understand their importance. The Reichstag Fire and the Enabling Law gave Hitler the opportunity to remove opposition to the Nazis - especially the communists. The Night of the Long Knives strengthened Hitler's position within the Nazi Party by eliminating the SA. The death of Hindenburg not only allowed Hitler to become Führer, but also gave him the support of the German army.

...*3*

History of the establishment of a Nazi Dictatorship

Events of February and March, 1933

Reichstag Fire

- After becoming Chancellor, Hitler called an election, so that he could increase Nazi seats in the Reichstag.
- On 27 February, the Reichstag building was burned down. A communist called Van Der Lubbe was caught inside the building.
- The fire gave Hitler the excuse to pass emergency laws to 'protect' the country from communists.
- Hitler banned the Communist Party from campaigning in the election.
- Some believed that the Nazis were responsible for the fire. This has never been proved.

March 1933 election and the Enabling Law

- In the election, the Nazis won 44 per cent of the vote (288 seats) but failed to get a majority.
- The Nationalist Party joined the Nazis and their 52 seats gave the Nazis a majority. However, it was below the 66 per cent needed to change the Constitution of the Geman Republic.
- The ban on the Communist Party meant that its 81 members could not take their seats in the Reichstag.

- Hitler then used the SA to threaten and bully other members of the Reichstag, such as the Social Democrats, to vote for the Enabling Law. This meant that the Enabling Law was passed.
- The Enabling Law gave Hitler complete power to make laws for four years, without consulting the Reichstag or the President. The Weimar constitution had been destroyed.

Summary box 1

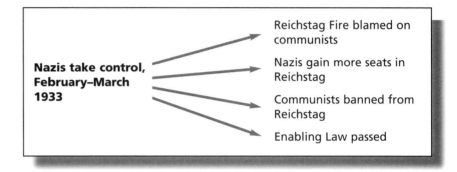

Removal of opposition

With the powers gained by the Enabling Law, Hitler now removed any opposition to the Nazi Party:

- Trade unions were abolished and their leaders arrested.
- The Social Democrat Party was banned.
- The Law against the Formation of New Parties banned all parties except the Nazis.
- Political opponents were arrested.
- Nazi ministers were appointed in national and state governments.
- Nazi supporters were appointed as civil servants and judges.

The Night of the Long Knives

- Hitler felt that the SA, under their leader Ernst Roehm, were becoming a threat to Hitler's control of the Nazi Party.
- The SA wanted more socialist policies than Hitler was prepared to accept. Hitler needed the support of big business and could not afford to lose its backing.
- The SA wanted control of the German army while Hitler wanted and needed the army's support.
- On 30 June Hitler ordered the murder of SA leaders, including Roehm. Other political opponents such as van Schleicher, the former Chancellor, were killed at the same time.

Death of Hindenburg

- On 2 August President Hindenburg died. Hitler declared himself the new President and took the title of Führer.
- The German army gave an oath of personal loyalty to Hitler, thus promising to serve him.
- Hitler and the Nazi Party now had complete control of Germany.

Summary box 2

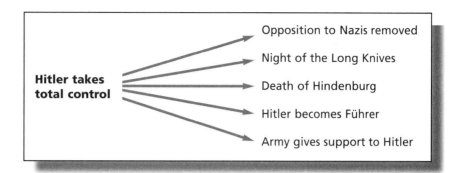

Hitler takes total control
- Opposition to Nazis removed
- Night of the Long Knives
- Death of Hindenburg
- Hitler becomes Führer
- Army gives support to Hitler

Key Dates To Learn

1933	January	Hitler becomes Chancellor
	February	Reichstag Fire
	March	Elections give Hitler control of the Reichstag
		Enabling Law
	May	Trade unions abolished
	June	All political parties except the Nazis are banned
1934	June	Night of the Long Knives eliminates the SA
	August	Death of President Hindenburg
		Hitler becomes Führer

4

What do I Know?

What is the importance of the following:
- The Enabling Law
- The Night of the Long Knives?

1 Who was blamed for the Reichstag Fire?

2 Which party was Hitler's ally in the Reichstag?

3 What did the Enabling Law allow Hitler to do?

4 Who did Hitler ban after the election of March 1933?

5 Who died on 2 August 1934?

6 What title did Hitler adopt after this?

7 Why was the army's oath of loyalty important to Hitler?

My score ......

5

Exam Type Question

Here is the sort of question you might be asked in Section B of Paper 2. Look closely at the answers given and the examiner's comments on them. Then answer the practice question.

> Describe the effects for Hitler of the removal of the SA in the Night of the Long Knives in June 1934.   **(5 marks)**

Answer 1

> The SA were killed in the Night of the Long Knives by members of the SS. This gave Hitler more power in the Nazi Party.

Answer 2

> The leaders of the SA and many of its members were removed on Hitler's orders by the SS in the Night of the Long Knives. The SA were becoming a threat to Hitler. They were unpopular with many Germans for their violence. They also had different ideas to Hitler – for example, they felt that they should control the army. So their removal strengthened Hitler's control of the Nazi Party. He knew that he could rely on the SS. The removal of the SA also made Hitler more popular in Germany. Businessmen disliked the socialist ideas of the SA. Above all, the army approved of this and now gave its support to Hitler.

Examiner's Comments: Answer 1

2 out of 5

A short – too short – answer that misses out most of the relevant detail. Did the candidate know very much about the Night of the Long Knives? However, there is some explanation – it gave Hitler more power in the Nazi Party. There is also one point of knowledge – the SS removed the SA. The answer therefore gets 2 marks.

Answer 2

5 out of 5

A good answer. It shows an understanding of the two key elements of the question – how removal of the SA strengthened Hitler within the Nazi Party and in Germany as a whole. The answer also provides knowledge to support the explanation. You might be able to find some gaps in the knowledge – for example, there is no mention of Roehm – but this answer would receive the maximum mark.

Practice Question

Now try to answer this sort of question yourself.

How did the Nazis use the Reichstag Fire to increase their power in Germany? **(5 marks)**

This is a short 'free-standing' knowledge question – that is, it does not have a source to help or guide you. It is the kind of question that can be found in Section B of Paper 2. It generally has a value of 5 marks. Remember the following:

1 It requires you to produce a short, relevant answer that shows knowledge of the event.

2 It is relatively easy – provided you have revised.

5.4 Nazi rule in Germany, 1934–39

1

Topic Summary

Between 1934 and 1939 Germany was a totalitarian state with the German people under the control of a Nazi dictatorship. The Nazis ruled through control and oppression, and persuasion and propaganda. Control was enforced by the SS and the Gestapo, and there was also control of education and censorship of the media. The Nazis also persecuted those Germans not accepted as true Aryans – especially the Jews. In some ways some Germans did benefit from Nazi rule, for example increased employment. However, this came at the loss of their freedom.

2

What do I Need to Know?

This topic covers a number of different areas. You will need to know how the Nazis exercised control in Germany by the use of the SS and the Gestapo, and by the persecution of different groups including the Jews. You will also need to understand how other methods of control were used – in education and the youth movement, and in censorship. You should be aware of the use of propaganda to keep the support of the German people. Finally, it is important to see that there were some benefits to some of the German people, especially in the creation of jobs – but they came at a heavy price.

3

History of Nazi rule in Germany, 1934–39

The Nazi dictatorship

A totalitarian or police state was created with Hitler and the Nazis in complete control.

Law and order

- The SS, under the control of Himmler, had unlimited powers, including powers of arrest.
- The Death Head Units of the SS ran the concentration camps where people could be sent without trial.
- The Gestapo (secret police) also had unlimited powers. Its officers could arrest people simply for criticising the Nazis.
- The Gestapo encouraged people to report on any 'anti-Nazi' activity by their neighbours, fellow workers, friends, even their own family.
- Judges were expected to support the ideas of the Nazi Party, rather than those of justice. 'Unreliable' judges were removed.

Persecution of the Jews

Once in power, Hitler put his anti-Semitic (anti-Jewish) ideas, outlined in *Mein Kampf*, into operation:

- In 1933 Jewish shops and businesses were boycotted.
- In 1934 any Jews who were employed as civil servants, teachers or in other government jobs were dismissed.
- Jews were banned from parks, public buildings and public transport.
- The Nuremberg Laws of 1935 took away Jews' rights as German citizens. Marriage between Jews and non-Jews was also banned.
- Many Jews now began to leave Germany.
- In November 1938 Jewish shops and synagogues were destroyed in *Kristallnacht* (the Night of Broken Glass). Thousands of Jews were arrested and during the next few weeks over 30,000 Jews were sent to concentration camps.
- **After 1939** the 'Final Solution', the extermination of Jewish people, began. This resulted in 6 million Jews being killed.

Persecution of other groups

- Anyone not considered to be an 'Aryan' suffered under the Nazis. This included gypsies and black people, who were considered inferior.
- People not 'socially useful', like tramps and mentally and physically disabled people, were also put into concentration camps.
- Churches also had to accept Nazi rule. Priests and ministers who did not, such as Martin Niemoller, were put into concentration camps.
- A Reich church, dominated by Nazis, was also set up.

Education and young people

- The Nazis completely controlled education in order to indoctrinate (brainwash) children into following Nazi ideas.
- All teachers had to be members of the Nazi Party. All lessons had to reflect Nazi ideas.
- Every child was taught to be fit and ready to fight for Germany. Physical education was a priority.
- Girls were taught how to be good wives and mothers.
- The Hitler Youth was set up to control how young people spent their leisure time. It indoctrinated them with Nazi ideas and stressed service to the Reich in the army or elsewhere. It wanted to ensure that children were loyal to Hitler.

Women

- Women were encouraged to have children. Schemes were introduced to 'reward' women for having children.
- Women were also encouraged to give up their jobs and stay at home to look after their husbands and children.
- Advice was given to women on what to wear and what to cook.

Censorship and propaganda

- Josef Goebbels was the Minister of Propaganda and Enlightenment. He controlled what Germans read and heard.
- Newspapers, films, books, art and music were all controlled and censored so that they supported Nazi ideas. As a result, many artists and writers left Germany.
- Radio broadcasts were controlled. Cheap radios were provided so that all Germans could hear Hitler's speeches at home, in factories, in shops and at school.
- Groups such as the Jews were always shown in a bad light.
- Mass rallies were held and used as propaganda events. The most famous was the Nuremberg rally, held every August.
- Hitler was portrayed as a great, almost god-like, figure.

Summary box 1

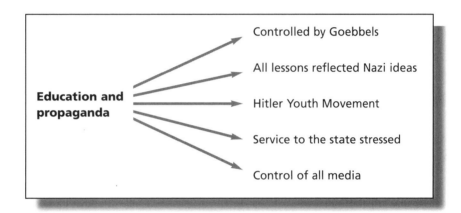

Economic policy

In 1933 there were 6 million unemployed in Germany. By 1938 fewer than half a million were without work. Hitler solved the problem of unemployment in a number of ways:

- Public works programmes such as building roads (autobahns), houses and public buildings were established.
- In 1935 rearmament began and men were conscripted into the armed forces.
- Rearmament created jobs in industries that supplied the armed forces.
- Aryan men replaced people such as Jews and women who were forced out of work and who were not then recorded as being unemployed. Jobs were also created by the growing numbers of people being sent to concentration camps.

Hitler also planned to make Germany self-sufficient in key products such as coal, oil and iron. This policy is called *autarky*. New, synthetic products such as textiles and petrol were also developed. Although some progress was made, these areas of economic policy were not successful.

Summary box 2

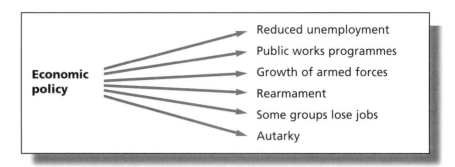

Work and leisure

- Hitler banned trade unions and made strikes illegal.
- The German Labour Front now controlled all workers, wages and hours of work. Pay usually went down and the hours of work became longer.
- 'Strength Through Joy' provided leisure activities to organise workers' free time. Workers were given sports facilities, cheap holidays and even Mediterranean cruises.
- There were plans to build the Volkswagen (People's Car) so that it was cheap enough for workers to afford.
- Workers were persuaded through propaganda that they were serving Germany.

Summary box 3

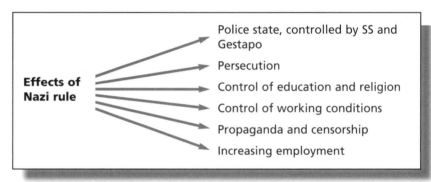

4

What do I Know?

What is the importance of the following:

- the Gestapo
- Propaganda
- Public works programmes
- Hitler Youth Movement?

1 What was the purpose of the Minister of Propaganda and Enlightenment?

2 Why was Hitler so keen to control education?

3 What was the SS?

4 Which laws of 1935 limited the rights of Jews?

5 What was *Kristallnacht*?

6 Give one way in which the Nazis reduced unemployment.

7 What is *autarky*?

8 Which organisation controlled German workers after 1934?

9 Which organisation organised leisure activities for the workers?

My score ......

5

Exam Type Question

Here is the sort of source-based question that can be found in either Section A or B of Paper 2, which carries higher marks (9 or 10). Look closely at the answer given and the examiner's comments. Then answer the practice question.

Source A

▼ Hitler youth reading *Der Sturmer*, a Nazi newspaper.

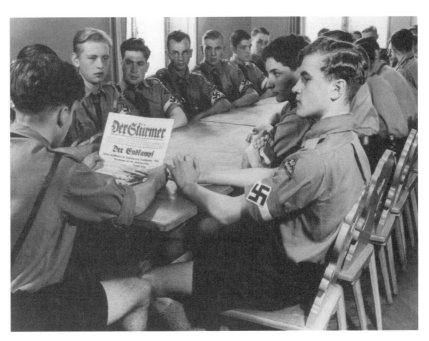

Source B

▼ Hitler youth in a chariot race.

How useful are the sources for learning about the Hitler Youth Movement? Explain your answer, using the sources and your own knowledge. **(9 marks)**

Answer

The sources are not really very useful. They show us what the Hitler Youth was like. They wore uniforms and played games like the chariot race shown in the photograph. However, the photos would have been taken by a Nazi to show the Hitler Youth in a good light so they are of limited use.

Examiner's Comments

3 out of 9

The candidate has tried to explain whether the sources are useful. However, the explanation is limited – the photos were biased and so not useful. There is description of the two photos but no evidence of any knowledge. To get higher marks, the candidate would need to suggest how the sources are useful despite their bias, and back up description of the sources with explanation and knowledge not found in the sources.

Practice Question

Now have a go at answering the above question yourself. Remember that it requires you to do two things:

1 Use the evidence in the sources to explain how useful they are.
2 Use your knowledge to support your answer. This can be done by mentioning something that is relevant to the sources and which helps to explain them – but which is not directly mentioned in the source.

The mark allocation for this question is 7 marks for analysis of the sources and 2 marks for supporting knowledge.

6 The USA, 1919–41

6.1 The growth of Isolation, 1919–22

1

Topic Summary

The First World War had brought benefits to the USA. America had supplied the Allies with their food and raw materials, and also gained overseas markets from the countries involved in the fighting. It had become the strongest power in the world. However, the war had other effects. The loss of American lives in a 'European' war brought a mood of isolation – of not wanting to get involved in the problems of other countries. This caused policy changes within the USA including the restriction of immigration and trade.

2

What do I Need to Know?

This is a short topic but there are some important issues that you need to know. The effects of the First World War on the USA should be understood: it brought a mood of isolation that resulted in the rejection of the Treaty of Versailles and the League of Nations. You also need to understand how this mood changed policy in the USA, with restrictions in immigration via the Immigration Quota Act of 1921. There were also policies to protect US markets by introducing taxes on foreign goods. For this, you should understand the Fordney–McCumber Tariff and its effects.

3

History of the growth of Isolation

Reaction in the USA to the First World War

- In April 1917, the USA joined the war on the Allied side. 100,000 Americans were killed.
- Early in 1918 President Wilson proposed the Fourteen Points to help preserve world peace.
- The mood in the USA was becoming isolationist. Many American people wanted to withdraw from world affairs; they did not want to be made to foot the bill to keep world peace.
- Many politicians, mostly Republicans, understood this mood. In 1920 they were elected to office.
- As a result, the USA rejected the Treaty of Versailles and did not join the League of Nations.

Summary box 1

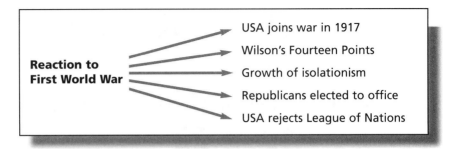

Reaction to First World War
- USA joins war in 1917
- Wilson's Fourteen Points
- Growth of isolationism
- Republicans elected to office
- USA rejects League of Nations

Restricting immigration

- The USA had been a country that welcomed immigrants from many countries. It was a land of opportunity – a place to get rich.
- Most immigrants had come from Europe and had helped the USA to become a great country.
- After 1918, the feeling towards immigration changed:
  - Many Americans were White, Anglo-Saxon Protestants (WASPs) but new immigrants included Catholics from Italy or Jews from Russia.
  - Immigrants from Russia were also thought to be communists. This 'Red Scare' worsened after the Bolshevik Revolution of 1917.
  - Immigrants were made to take a literacy test in English before entering the country. As many immigrants from poorer countries were illiterate this prevented them from entering the USA.
  - Many immigrants were willing to work for lower pay than US citizens.
- The Immigration Quota Act was passed in 1921. It set a quota of 357,000 immigrants allowed into the USA each year. In addition, the quota stated that the number of people emigrating from a country should total no more than 3 per cent of the people from that country already living in the USA in 1910. This favoured immigrants from northern and western Europe because most immigrants had come from these regions before 1910.
- In 1924 the quota changed to 2 per cent of the 1890 population. This again favoured immigrants from countries such as Britain and Germany.
- No immigrants from Asia were admitted.

Summary box 2

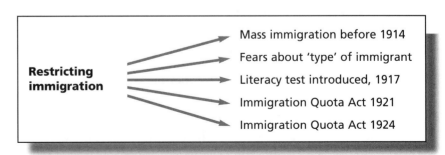

Restricting immigration
- Mass immigration before 1914
- Fears about 'type' of immigrant
- Literacy test introduced, 1917
- Immigration Quota Act 1921
- Immigration Quota Act 1924

Tariff controls: 'economic isolation'

- US business had prospered in the First World War and had gained new markets.
- After the war European countries tried to sell their goods in the USA.
- American business people knew that they could not sell many goods in Europe because Europe was still recovering from war.
- The Fordney–McCumber Tariff of 1922 set tariffs (taxes) on foreign goods entering the USA to 'protect' US goods.
- Tariffs made US goods cheaper than foreign goods so sales of home-produced goods increased.

However,

- Foreign countries retaliated by putting tariffs on US goods entering their countries. This hit American farmers and older industries, such as textiles and coal, that needed to sell goods abroad.

Summary box 3

Key Dates To Learn

1917	The USA enters First World War
	Literacy test introduced for all immigrants
1918	First World War ends
1920	The USA rejects Treaty of Versailles and League of Nations
1921	Immigration Quota Act
1922	Fordney–McCumber Tariff Act
1924	Immigration Quota Act

4 What do I Know?

1 In which year did the USA enter the First World War?

2 What were the Fourteen Points?

3 What organisation did the USA refuse to join in 1920?

4 What was the quota system for immigrants in 1921?

5 What was the quota system in 1924?

6 What is the system that protects industry from foreign competition?

My score ......

What is the importance of the following:

- Isolationism
- Tariff control?

5

Exam Type Question

Here is the sort of source-based question you might be asked in Section A of Paper 2. Look closely at the answer given and the examiner's comments. Then answer the practice question.

Maximum number of immigrants allowed	357,000	All countries
Number of immigrants allowed from each country	77,342	Britain
	68,059	Germany
	42,957	Italy
	34,284	Russia
	32,244	Sweden and Norway
	25,827	Poland
	14,382	Czechoslovakia
	62,095	Other countries

▲ **The Immigration Act of 1921: it limited the number of immigrants to 3 per cent of the 1910 population in the USA.**

> What can you learn from the source about the immigration policy of the USA in 1921? **(5 marks)**

Answer

Immigration to the USA went down. It was limited to 3 per cent of the 1910 population. So only 357,000 immigrants were allowed in.

Examiner's Comments

2 out of 5
This is a rather simple answer. However, it does show a basic understanding – immigration went down. And it provides evidence to support that understanding – the limit of 357,000. The 3 per cent limit is not well explained. The two points covered earn the answer 2 marks.

6

Practice Question

Now have a go at answering the question above. Remember the question requires you to examine a source and draw conclusions from that source. No additional knowledge is needed and your answer should cover only what is in the source.

6.2 The Promised Land? The USA in the 1920s

...1
Topic Summary

The 1920s was a time of contrasts in the USA. Economic prosperity allowed many Americans to buy a wide range of consumer goods to make life easier. They also began to invest in shares, and the stock market boomed. At the same time there was poverty, and many Americans could not share in the prosperity. There was also intolerance, especially towards black people. In addition, the introduction of Prohibition resulted in organised crime and violence.

...2
What do I Need to Know?

You will need to know why the USA became so prosperous in the 1920s. There is not just one reason, but a number of reasons which came together at the same time – mass production and mechanisation, government policies, increased credit and hire purchase, and growth in the stock market. However, you should remember that not every American could benefit from the boom. You must also be aware that there was a darker side to the USA. Organisations like the Ku Klux Klan (KKK) persecuted black people; prohibition brought with it gangsters and organised crime.

...3
History of the USA in the 1920s

Economic prosperity

Reasons for economic prosperity

- Mass production and the assembly line allowed goods to be made quicker and cheaper. Production rose rapidly.
- The motor car industry is the best example of the use of mass production (Henry Ford's company was the first to use it). This also helped other industries to grow, such as oil, steel, rubber.
- Mass production was also used in consumer goods industries such as washing machines and telephones.
- The tariff policy of the government protected industries from foreign competition (see Section 6.1).
- Low taxes and credit facilities such as hire purchase meant that Americans had money to spend on goods.
- All this created 'confidence' that encouraged Americans to buy goods.
- Americans invested in companies by buying shares. They bought shares 'on the margin', paying back loans when share prices went up.

Summary box 1

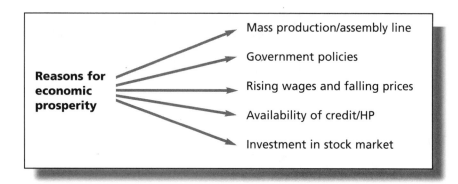

Features of economic prosperity

- Increase in production of cars and consumer goods such as radios, fridges, washing machines and vacuum cleaners.
- Fall in prices of these goods.
- Increase in average wages in the USA.
- Easy credit and hire purchase to buy goods.
- Use of advertising to encourage people to buy these new goods, to 'keep up with the Joneses'.

Americans who did not share in the prosperity

Some sections of the population continued to live in poverty:

- **Farmers.** New machinery produced too much food – more than the US population needed – so food prices fell. This meant that farmers' incomes fell, and many farmers were evicted from their land because they could not afford to keep up their mortgage payments.
- **Black people.** Many black people suffered from the slump in farming and lost their jobs. Large numbers moved from the south to the north in search of work but still ended up with the lowest-paid jobs. This was also the case for many immigrants.
- **Workers in older industries.** Coalmines closed as people began using new forms of power such as gas, oil and electricity. Textile factories closed as demand fell.

Ku Klux Klan and racism

- The KKK was a secret group, active mainly in the south. Members were often poor white people who did not share in the boom, and who felt that immigrants and black people threatened their jobs because they were willing to work for lower wages.
- The KKK believed that the only true Americans were WASPs – White, Anglo-Saxon and Protestant. It opposed all other groups such as black people, Jews, Catholics and immigrants from Asia and southern and eastern Europe.
- Black people were the main target of the KKK because it believed that black people were inferior to white people. It committed violent crimes against them including public lynching, murder and destruction of property.

- Klan members often got away with their crimes because the Klan had links with the police and judges. It would also threaten witnesses and juries.
- It forced many black people to move to the northern towns.
- By the late 1920s its membership began to fall – but it continues to exist.

Summary box 2

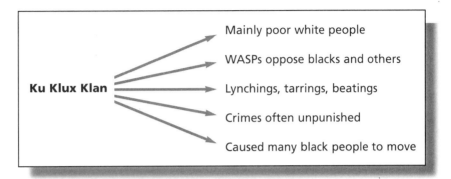

Ku Klux Klan

- Mainly poor white people
- WASPs oppose blacks and others
- Lynchings, tarrings, beatings
- Crimes often unpunished
- Caused many black people to move

Prohibition and organised crime

Prohibition

- The campaign against the evils of drink was led by temperance groups who claimed that alcohol brought poverty and caused crime and destruction.
- The Volstead Act 1920 banned the making, selling and transporting of alcoholic drink – this was Prohibition.
- Most Americans opposed Prohibition and were prepared to break the law to continue drinking.
- Moonshine (illegal drink) was manufactured; speakeasies (illegal bars) were established.
- Bootleggers smuggled alcohol from other countries: rum from the West Indies and whisky from Canada.
- Attempts by the authorities to control the illegal drink trade failed.
- In 1933 Roosevelt ended Prohibition.

Organised crime

- Gangsters began to control the illegal alcohol industry in the cities.
- Soon other rackets (illegal enterprises) developed – protection, drugs and prostitution.
- Rival gangs fought for control of territory, resulting in an increase in gangland murders, for example the St Valentine's Day Massacre 1929.
- Al Capone emerged as the most powerful gangster in Chicago and was famous throughout the USA.
- Judges and the police were often bribed to ignore the gangsters' activities.
- The number of gangsters declined once Prohibition ended.

Summary box 3

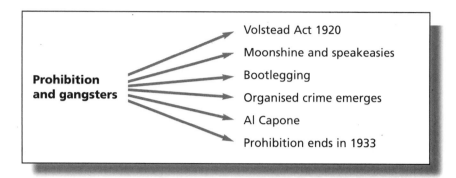

Prohibition and gangsters

- Volstead Act 1920
- Moonshine and speakeasies
- Bootlegging
- Organised crime emerges
- Al Capone
- Prohibition ends in 1933

Entertainment and flappers: the Roaring Twenties

- A result of the boom was that Americans wanted to spend more money on being entertained, going to nightclubs and buying clothes.
- Most homes had radios, which broadcast adverts for new consumer goods.
- Jazz became very popular and was often played in the speakeasies. It was seen as new and daring.
- The cinema became popular, with Hollywood at the centre of the film industry. Actors such as Charlie Chaplin and Rudolph Valentino became celebrities.
- Young women became 'flappers' with short skirts and short hair.

4

What do I Know?

What is important about the following:
- Mass production
- Prohibition
- The Ku Klux Klan?

1 Who first introduced mass production in the USA?

2 How did the car industry help other industries to grow?

3 What was Prohibition?

4 What were 'speakeasies' and 'moonshine'?

5 Who was the leading gangster in Chicago?

6 What is meant by the initials WASP?

7 Name two groups of people hated by the Ku Klux Klan.

8 Who were the 'flappers'?

My score ......

5

Exam Type Question

Here is the sort of short essay question you will be asked in Sections A and B of Paper 2. Look closely at the answer given and the examiner's comments on it.

Explain how the USA achieved economic prosperity in the 1920s. **(15 marks)**

Answer

During the 1920s the USA was prosperous. There are a number of reasons for this.

Mass production, which meant that goods were produced on the assembly line, was most important. Goods could be produced faster and cheaper. Prices for them fell so more Americans could buy them. The car industry with Henry Ford was the first to use mass production but other products could be made like this – washing machines, radios, vacuum cleaners.

People also found it easier to buy goods. Employment was high and taxes were low. There was credit and hire purchase to let people buy goods over a long period of time. They were also pressured into buying things by advertising and keeping up with the Joneses.

The American people were also confident. They had jobs and good wages. They began to buy shares in companies, borrowing the money from banks. The value of shares went up and up and this made people even richer.

So Americans became prosperous. But it did not last long. The Wall Street Crash brought Depression in 1929.

Examiner's Comments

12 out of 15

This is a good answer but there are some areas where it could be improved. Of the five reasons for prosperity, three are covered – mass production, credit and confidence. These are given in detail and show plenty of understanding. Of the other two reasons, one is not mentioned at all – the effects of war. The other is mentioned only in passing – the government policy of low taxes; but there is no mention of tariff controls and their effects. The final two paragraphs are good and show that the candidate has a firm understanding of the topic.

The answer is strong enough for 12 out of 15 marks. See if you can add a sentence on the two missing areas to gain the extra marks.

Practice Question

Now try to answer this sort of question yourself.

Explain how prohibition and organised crime affected the lives of the American people in the 1920s. **(15 marks)**

Look back to page 119 for hints on answering this type of short essay question.

6.3 The USA in Depression, 1929–33

1

Topic Summary

In 1929 the economic prosperity, which many Americans thought would last indefinitely, suddenly ended. It gave way to Depression brought about by the Wall Street Crash. Unemployment grew and millions of Americans found themselves reduced to a state of poverty – homeless and dependent on charity to survive. The Republican government could do little to solve their problems.

2

What do I Need to Know?

You will need to recognise the reasons that brought Depression to the USA. Some of these are long term – that is, they existed even in the 1920s prosperity. They include the poverty of many Americans and the tariff policy of the government (mentioned in Section 6.2). The other reason for Depression is short term – the Wall Street Crash. You will need to understand how the collapse of share prices led to Depression and the effects of the Depression – unemployment, homelessness and reliance on charity. You should also examine the actions of the Republican government in trying to deal with the Depression and understand how its failures led to the election of Roosevelt in 1932.

3

History of the Depression

Causes of the Depression

- **Poverty.** More than half the population were too poor to share in the prosperity of the 1920s. They lived 'below the poverty line'. They included black workers, farmers and new immigrants.
- **Overproduction.** Because of mass production, more goods were produced than could be sold – the market became saturated. This forced factories to shut and workers to become unemployed. It led to a 'cycle of depression'.
- **Tariff policy.** When the USA placed tariffs on foreign imports in the early 1920s, foreign governments retaliated by placing tariffs on US goods. This meant that foreign markets for US goods could not be found.
- **Speculation.** Americans bought shares in the 1920s on credit and expected a profit – speculation. When the value of shares did not rise in 1928, people began to sell their shares and the value of shares fell.
- **The Wall Street Crash** in 1929 brought the collapse of the stock market as the value of shares crashed.

Summary box 1

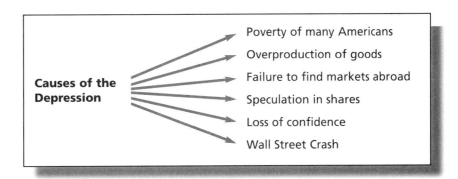

The Wall Street Crash and its effects

- On Thursday, 24 October 1929 ('Black Thursday'), the stock market 'collapsed' as investors tried to sell more and more of their shares. Share prices dropped. On 28 and 29 October, share values fell even more.
- Thousands of people were ruined. Many were speculators who only bought and sold shares for money.
- Banks now called in loans from people who had borrowed money to buy shares. When people could not pay back the loans, they were forced into bankruptcy.
- This put pressure on banks, which had also invested in shares. People with money in banks began to panic and withdraw their money – this created a 'run on the banks'.
- Businesses shut down as their shares became valueless and banks called in loans.
- Unemployment grew as businesses closed. This meant that fewer people could buy goods and resulted in more businesses closing.
- A vicious circle was created – a cycle of depression.

Summary box 2

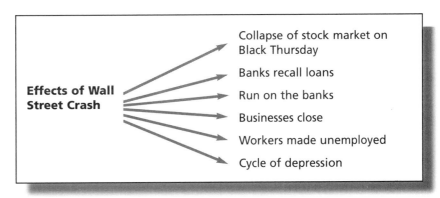

The effects of the Depression

- Unemployment increased, especially in the northern towns. In 1928, 1.6 million people were unemployed; by 1933, this figure had risen to 14 million.
- Americans travelled the country to look for work. These people were called 'hobos'.
- Americans lost their homes because they could not afford to keep up their mortgage payments.

- Shanty towns, known as 'Hoovervilles' as an insult to President Hoover, were set up by the homeless on waste ground in towns.
- The unemployed relied on charity kitchens for soup and bread, queuing in 'breadlines'.
- Farmers continued to suffer as prices of farm produce fell. Prices fell so low that it became unprofitable even to harvest the crops: wheat was left to rot in the field.
- The 'dust bowl' brought added problems. The land had been overfarmed and became infertile. Drought followed, which turned the soil into dust. Farms were abandoned.

Summary box 3

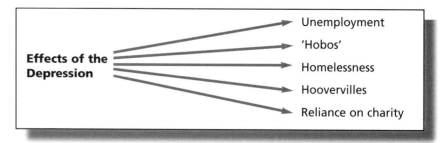

The Republican government and the Depression

- Herbert Hoover had been elected President in 1928 on the promise that prosperity would continue.
- When the Depression came, Hoover believed that it would end by itself – without any government interference.
- Republicans believed in 'rugged individualism' (that people should help themselves). So there was no state benefit for the unemployed.
- Some actions were taken by the government to create jobs (for example, the Hoover Dam was built), but they were not enough to help the large numbers of people who had been made unemployed.
- Hoover and the Republicans were blamed for the Depression. People said: 'In Hoover we trusted, now we are busted.'
- A campaign by the Bonus Army – ex-soldiers who wanted their pensions early – increased Hoover's unpopularity. Armed troops with tanks and tear gas were sent in to clear the Bonus Army during its protest against the government.
- In the 1932 elections, American voters turned to the Democrats and Roosevelt.

Summary box 4

4

What do I Know?

What is important about the following:
- The Wall Street Crash
- Hoovervilles?

1 What caused overproduction in the 1920s?

2 What is the name given to buying shares for profit?

3 What happened on Black Thursday, 24 October 1929?

4 What happens when there is a 'run on the banks'?

5 Why were breadlines set up in the Depression?

6 What were 'hobos'?

7 Why didn't Hoover do more to help the unemployed?

My score ......

5

Exam Type Question

Here is the sort of source-based question that can be found in Section B of Paper 2. It generally carries 7 marks: 5 marks for knowledge and 2 marks for use of the source. Look closely at the answer given and the examiner's comments. Then answer the practice question.

▲ A Hooverville in Central Park, New York, in 1932.

Using the source and your knowledge, explain how the Depression affected the lives of many Americans. **(7 marks)**

Answer

> In the Depression many Americans were forced to live in Hoovervilles. These were shanty towns built on waste land in the centre of cities like New York. People who were forced out of their homes went to live in them.

Examiner's Comments:

3 out of 7

This is a limited answer. It confines itself very much to the source. Part of the answer is only a description of the source. However there is some knowledge – the candidate recognises that Hoovervilles are shanty towns and explains why people may have had to live in them. To get a better mark, the candidate would need to show background knowledge of Hoovervilles - why they were set up, and link Hoovervilles to the effects of the Depression - unemployment, begging, reliance on charity etc.

6

Practice Question

> On the outskirts of the cities and on empty plots there were groups of makeshift shacks made out of packing boxes, scrap iron, anything that could be picked up free from the city dumps. Men and, sometimes, whole families of evicted people were sleeping on car seats from scrapyards, warming themselves before fires of rubbish in oil drums.

▲ From *Since Yesterday* by F L Allen, published in 1939.

Is the source an accurate interpretation of the effects of the Depression on the American people?
Use the source and your own knowledge to answer the question. **(10 marks)**

This is the kind of question found in Section A of Paper 2. It has one of the higher marks (9 or 10 marks) and so it is one of the more difficult questions you will have to face. It requires you to do two things:

• Evaluate or understand the source to explain if it is accurate.

• Use your knowledge to support your answer.

The mark allocation for this question is 7 marks for evaluation of the source and 3 marks for supporting knowledge. Your answer should reflect this allocation.

6.4 Recovery from Depression, 1933–41

Topic Summary

In 1932 the American people elected Roosevelt as their President to take them out of the Depression. He offered a different approach to solving the problems caused by the Depression – a New Deal to bring 'relief, recovery and reform'. Many of these actions were successful but not all Americans supported them. Historians also disagree as to whether it was the New Deal or the Second World War that ended the Depression in the USA.

What do I Need to Know?

First, you will need to understand what the New Deal tried to do and how this was different from the policies of the previous Hoover government. You will need to know the details of the actions taken by Roosevelt to help banking, agriculture, industry and the unemployed. You should be aware of which Americans opposed the New Deal and why. Finally, you will need to consider the effects of the New Deal – did it manage to bring the USA out of Depression?

History of the recovery from the Depression

The 1932 election

- Hoover and the Republicans believed that the Depression would soon end on its own and that no further action was needed.
- Roosevelt and the Democrats promised a 'New Deal for the American people'. The government would intervene to provide jobs and bring recovery to the economy.
- Roosevelt won a convincing victory in the election for President: 42 out of the 48 states in the USA supported him.

The Hundred Days: early actions by Roosevelt

- Roosevelt told the American people that 'the only thing to fear is fear itself' and that the Depression could be overcome.
- Roosevelt was granted emergency powers by Congress to take quick action.
- Roosevelt then passed fifteen new laws setting up government agencies to deal with agriculture and unemployment (the Alphabet Agencies, see p. 150-51).
- The Emergency Banking Act was passed in 1933. All banks were closed for four days so that government officials could inspect their books. Only well-managed banks were allowed to reopen. This restored people's confidence in banks and they began to put their money in them again.

- Roosevelt tried to reassure the American people by using 'fireside chats'. These were radio broadcasts in which he sat in a chair by the fire in his office and spoke to the people about the Depression and what he was doing about it. The first fireside chat was about banking and he persuaded the people to put their money back into banks. Roosevelt continued with his fireside chats throughout his time as President.
- These actions helped to restore confidence in the USA and earned Roosevelt the trust of the American people.

Summary box 1

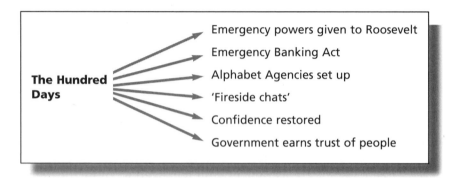

The Hundred Days
- Emergency powers given to Roosevelt
- Emergency Banking Act
- Alphabet Agencies set up
- 'Fireside chats'
- Confidence restored
- Government earns trust of people

The New Deal

Aim of the New Deal

Roosevelt aimed to turn the 'cycle of depression' (see Section 6.3) into a 'cycle of recovery'. This would be done by the government putting money into the economy to provide jobs. People would then have money to spend and so could buy more goods. This in turn would create more jobs to produce these goods.

Roosevelt summed up the aims of the New Deal as:

- **Relief.** Help to the poor and the homeless.
- **Recovery.** Help to industry to provide jobs.
- **Reform.** Help to the old, unemployed, sick and others in need.

The Alphabet Agencies

- AAA (Agricultural Adjustment Act) limited the amount of food produced by farmers. This reduced the supply of food and so prices rose. If a farmer lost money by this, the government made up the loss. So farmers were being paid to produce less.
- FERA (Federal Emergency Relief Administration) was set up in 1933 to provide quick relief for the hungry, homeless and unemployed.
- CWA (Civil Works Administration) created 4 million jobs in 1933–34 via public works schemes. Many of these jobs were short-term – they lasted for only a short time.
- PWA (Public Works Administration) created jobs in public works schemes, such as building schools and hospitals. These were more permanent jobs but they often required skilled labour.

- WPA (Works Progress Administration) was similar to the PWA. It provided jobs for 2 million people building roads, bridges, schools and so on.
- TVA (Tennessee Valley Authority) was set up to help one of the poorest regions of the USA. Dams were built along the Tennessee River so that it did not flood and destroy crops and houses. The dams also produced cheap hydroelectricity. New industries were attracted to the area and leisure activities took place on the lakes. All this created jobs in the area.
- CCC (Civilian Conservation Corps) provided jobs for young unemployed men in the countryside, to improve the environment.
- NRA (National Recovery Administration) encouraged companies to set a minimum wage and maximum hours of work for its workers and to set fair prices. Any company that was part of the scheme could put a 'blue eagle' symbol on its products. Americans were then encouraged to buy these goods.
- HOLC (Home Owners Loan Corporation) helped people in difficulty with their mortgage payments.
- In 1935 the Social Security Act set up a scheme to provide pensions for the old, for widows and for the sick. It also set up unemployment benefit.
- In 1935 the Wagner Act gave Americans the right to join and form trade unions.

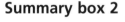

Summary box 2

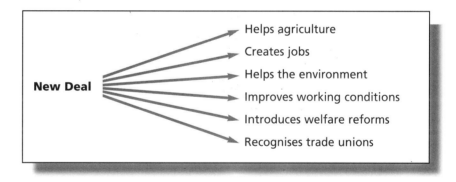

Opposition to the New Deal

Despite Roosevelt's massive election victories in 1932 and 1936, not everyone agreed with the New Deal:

- Republicans objected to the high cost of the New Deal and the increased taxes needed to pay for it. They still believed in 'rugged individualism' and felt that people should look after themselves. Many Republicans also thought that Roosevelt was acting like a dictator.
- Business people objected to government interference in, for example, the rights given to workers and the recognition given to trade unions.

- The Supreme Court, the highest court in the USA, decided that some of the agencies were unconstitutional – they went against the rights of the American people. For example, the NRA's action to improve the conditions of workers was seen to be against the rights of employers. The AAA was also declared illegal. After his 1936 election victory, Roosevelt tried to add six judges to the Supreme Court so that it would have a Democrat majority. However, this was unpopular with many Americans. In the end, Roosevelt and the Supreme Court backed down.
- Radicals such as Huey Long of Louisiana thought that Roosevelt was not doing enough. They wanted higher taxes on the rich and more help for the poor.

Summary box 3

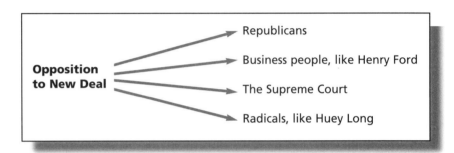

The effects of the New Deal

Was it a success?

- The New Deal created jobs for millions of Americans who had suffered in the Depression.
- It developed confidence in the American economy again.
- Some measures like the TVA and the Social Security Act had lasting effects.

However,

- Many Americans did not benefit from the New Deal – black people and farmers, for example.
- It was less effective in the late 1930s and unemployment began to rise after 1937.

The effects of the Second World War

- In the late 1930s the fall in employment came about mainly through the build-up to war.
- Roosevelt started a lend–lease policy: goods were provided to the Allies on credit, to be paid after the war. This helped boost US industry and farming.
- The USA entered the war in December 1941. The growth of the US army, and its provision with weapons, uniforms and so on, greatly reduced unemployment.

4

What do I Know?

What is important about the following:
- Fireside chats
- Alphabet Agencies
- The TVA?

1 Which political party did Roosevelt belong to?
2 What did the Emergency Banking Act 1933 do?
3 Name one Alphabet Agency that created jobs for Americans.
4 What does TVA stand for?
5 What did the CCC do?
6 Name two groups that opposed the New Deal.
7 Why did the Supreme Court reject some of the measures of the New Deal?
8 Why did the coming of the Second World War in 1939 increase employment in the USA?
9 When did the USA enter the Second World War?

My score ......

5

Exam Type Question

Here is the sort of source-based question you might be asked in Section A of Paper 2. The mark allocation is 7 marks for evaluation of the source and 3 marks for supporting knowledge. Look closely at the answer given and the examiner's comments. Then answer the practice question.

> Dear Mr President, this is just to tell you everything is alright now. The man you sent went down to the bank with us and the mortgage can go on for a while longer. You remember I wrote about losing the furniture too. Well, your man got it back for us. I never heard of a President like you, Mr Roosevelt. Mrs _____ and I are old folks and don't amount to much, but we are joined by millions of others in praying for you every night. God bless you, Mr Roosevelt.

▲ **Letter written to President Roosevelt.**

Is the source an accurate interpretation of the effects of the New Deal? Use the source and your own knowledge to answer the question. **(10 marks)**

Answer

The source tells us how grateful this old couple are to Roosevelt for saving their home. It is a letter so we should be able to tell if it is genuine. However, there is very little detail about the letter. We are not told when it was written or where it was written from – it might be from an area that did well in the New Deal. We don't know if this was the only letter like this that Roosevelt received. We are also not told who published it – so it might be biased. So although the source can be accurate in telling us about the New Deal, we do need to know much more about it.

Examiner's Comments

6 out of 10

The first sentence only describes the source. It does not try to evaluate it. If the answer had ended here it would only have reached the lowest level (1 mark). The answer then goes on to examine the source in detail and offers a number of points about the accuracy of the source. The answer covers the first requirement of this type of question – it evaluates the source. However, there is no supporting evidence and so the second requirement has been omitted. This limits the mark awarded.

Now see if you can write a sentence of two that provides supporting knowledge and gains the missing marks.

Practice Question

Now try to answer this question.

Source A

The New Deal never demonstrated that it could achieve prosperity and left many problems unsolved. As late as 1941 there were 6 million unemployed Americans and not until the war did the army of jobless disappear.

▲ From *Roosevelt and the New Deal* by W E Leuchtenburg, published in 1963.

Source B

The New Deal did not cure the Depression but it did have many positive achievements. Schools, hospitals, railway stations, bridges, etc were all built. But far more significant was the simple fact that the New Deal restored hope to millions of men and women by providing them with a job.

▲ From *Franklin Roosevelt* by C P Hill, published in 1966.

Do Sources A and B agree about the success of Roosevelt's New Deal? **(6 marks)**

This is the kind of question found in Section A of Paper 2. It has a value of 5 or 6 marks. It requires you to look at the two sources and compare them, to explain the ways in which they are similar and the ways in which they are different. No additional knowledge is needed and your answer should only cover what is in the sources.

7 Britain, 1905–51

7.1 Britain, 1905–19: A Changing Society?

Topic Summary

In 1905 a Liberal government came to power. In the next ten years, a series of important reforms were introduced. The Liberals tackled social problems such as health and poverty. They brought in reforms to help children, the old, the sick and the unemployed. These new benefits needed to be paid for and this brought the Liberal government into conflict with the House of Lords in the 1909 Budget. This resulted in the Parliament Act of 1911. Other changes were also brewing in this period: the Suffragette movement was demanding the vote for women; and a new political party, the Labour Party, was beginning to emerge.

What do I Need to Know?

First, you need to know details of the social reform introduced by the Liberals: school meals and school medical inspections; old age pensions; National Insurance and its two parts, dealing with health and unemployment. Next, you need to understand the conflict between the Liberal government and the House of Lords. This requires you to know the details of the People's Budget of 1909 and of the Parliament Act of 1911. Finally, there are two shorter topics that you should be aware of. One is the Suffragette movement and its demand for votes for women; the other is the beginning of the Labour Party. By 1918 both had had some success: women over 30 had gained the vote and the Labour Party had 59 seats in Parliament.

History of Britain, 1905–19

The Welfare State

Two important surveys showed that there was much poverty in Britain: one was carried out by Charles Booth in London, the other by Seebohm Rowntree in York. The Liberal government was determined to do something about this, by introducing reforms that gave the state the responsibility for helping people in need – that is, by creating a Welfare State.

Children

- The Education (Provision of School Meals) Act 1906 allowed local authorities to pay for school meals for the poorest children. In 1914 this became compulsory.

- School medical inspections were introduced in 1907. Every child was to be examined by a doctor at least once a year. School clinics were also set up.

Old Age Pensions Act 1908

- Before 1908 elderly people had to look after themselves or be looked after by their sons and daughters. Otherwise they had to go into a workhouse.
- The full pension was paid to all people over 70 years on incomes of less than £21 a year.
- Pensions were paid on a sliding scale depending on the person's income. The highest pension payment was 5 shillings (25p) a week.
- The money for pensions came from government funds – that is, it was a 'non-contributory' scheme.
- By 1914 there were almost 1 million pensioners.

Labour Exchange Act 1909

- This Act allowed people looking for work to go to one place to see what jobs were available in the area, rather than going from factory to factory. Today labour exchanges are called job centres.

National Insurance Act 1911

Health insurance:

- Insurance against illness was available for all male workers earning less than £160 a year.
- This was a 'contributory' scheme. Each worker paid 4d a week; each employer paid 3d a week for every employee; and the state paid 2d a week for every worker. So 9d a week for each worker was paid into the scheme.
- When a worker became ill, he could claim 10 shillings (50p) a week for 26 weeks.
- In 1920 the scheme was extended to cover more people, including women.

Insurance against unemployment:

- Insurance against unemployment was for workers in industries where short-term unemployment was common such as shipbuilding, construction and engineering.
- This was a 'contributory' scheme. Workers, employers and the state each contributed $2\frac{1}{2}$d a week. So $7\frac{1}{2}$d a week for each worker was paid into the scheme.
- A worker who became unemployed received benefit of 7 shillings (35p) a week for up to fifteen weeks in a year.
- In 1920 the scheme was extended to cover more workers.

Summary box 1

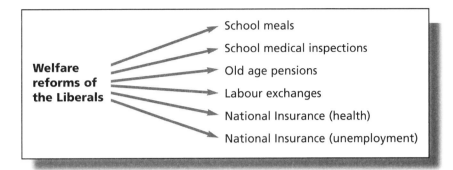

Conflict with the House of Lords: the constitutional crisis

The People's Budget 1909
The Liberal reforms cost money, especially old age pensions. This meant that the government needed extra revenue. The 1909 Budget proposed a number of ways to raise this money:

- Increase in income tax on the rich.
- Increase in death duties.
- Land tax on the profit made when land was sold.
- Increase in the taxes on tobacco and alcohol.

The Budget was popular, although not with wealthy people. It passed through the House of Commons but the House of Lords, which consisted mainly of rich people, rejected it. The Liberals then called a general election which took place in 1910. After the Liberals won this, the Budget was accepted by the House of Lords.

Parliament Act 1911
Once the struggle with the Budget was over, the Liberals were determined to reduce the power of the House of Lords. They promised to do this in the Parliament Bill:

- The Lords could not reject a money bill like a budget passed by the Commons.
- The Lords could reject other bills only twice.
- A general election would take place every five years rather than every seven.
- A further reform paid MPs for the first time.
- The House of Lords was forced to accept these changes when the King gave his support to the Liberal government.

Summary box 2

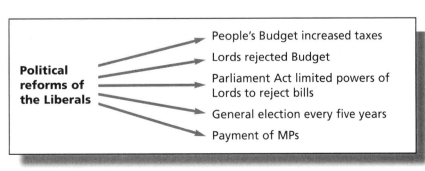

Votes for women

- The Women's Social and Political Union (WSPU), known as 'the Suffragettes', was set up to campaign for the right of women to vote.
- The methods they used were peaceful at first, but then became more violent.
- When arrested, Suffragettes went on hunger strike. This forced the government to pass the 'Cat and Mouse Act' in 1913: women on hunger strike were released until they recovered and then could be rearrrested.
- From 1914 to 1918 women played an important part in the war effort at home and in the armed forces. They changed their slogan from 'Right to Vote' to 'Right to Serve'.
- In 1918 women over 30 were given the vote.
- In 1928 women over 21 were given the vote – the same as for men.

The rise of the Labour Party: a time chart

1892	Keir Hardie elected as the first Labour MP
1893	Independent Labour Party formed to win more seats in Parliament
1906	29 Labour MPs elected after agreement with Liberals
1911	Payment of MPs helps the working-class Labour Party, who have few other sources of income
1913	Trade Union Act allows trade unions to fund the Labour Party
1918	59 Labour MPs elected Votes for men over 21 and women over 30 boosts support for the Labour Party
1924	First Labour government is formed

4

What do I Know?

What is important about the following:

- The Welfare State
- The Parliament Act 1911
- Suffragettes?

1 Name two reforms of the Liberals that helped children.
2 At what age would a person receive an old age pension in 1908?
3 What does '9d for 4d' mean in relation to the National Insurance Act 1911?
4 What kind of worker benefited from unemployment insurance?
5 Give one item in the Budget of 1909 that the rich opposed.
6 What was the Parliament Act of 1911?
7 Who got the vote in 1918?
8 Why did the payment of MPs help the Labour Party?

My score …

5

Exam Type Question

Here is the sort of source-based question you might be asked in Section A of the exam paper. It requires students to examine the source and draw conclusions from that source. No additional knowledge is needed. Look closely at the answer given and the examiner's comments.

▼ A Liberal government poster.

> What can you learn from the source about the welfare reforms of the Liberal government, 1905 to 1916?　　**(5 marks)**

Answer

The poster shows that National Insurance introduced by the Liberal government will help a worker when he is sick or disabled. The idea behind this and the Welfare State, is for the government to help people when they are unable to help themselves. This is shown by the man in bed being helped by another man, Lloyd George, who is the government. At the top of the poster it says 'The Dawn of Hope'. This suggests that the National Insurance reform is a big improvement on what was available before.

Examiner's
Comments:

5 out of 5

The answer shows a basic understanding of the purpose of the source in the first sentence. Then it goes on to develop that understanding by looking at the worker needing help and the government or state providing that help. The last two sentences are good. It shows that the candidate has used the whole source and has reached a valid conclusion on it. Note that when you look at a visual source, you should always remember to read the heading and the description of the source. You can often pick up additional information from them.

6

Practice Question

> When old age pensions began, life for the old was transformed. They were relieved of anxiety. They were suddenly rich. They were independent. At first when they went to the Post Office, tears of gratitude would run down the cheeks of some and they would say, as they picked up their money, 'God bless that Lord George'.

▲ From *Lark Rise to Candleford* by Flora Thompson, published in 1939.

Use the source and your knowledge to explain how the introduction of Old Age Pensions in 1908 helped old people in Britain. **(7 marks)**

This is the kind of question that can be found in Section B of Paper 2. It requires you to do two things:

- Use the evidence in the source to answer the question.
- Use your knowledge to explain the answer.

The mark allocation for this type of question is 5 marks for knowledge and 2 marks for using the evidence in the source. Make sure your answer reflects this allocation.

7.2 Britain, 1919–29: a case study of the General Strike

Topic Summary

In 1926 there was a General Strike in Britain. The causes go back to the periods before and after the First World War when there was much industrial unrest, especially in the old industries such as coalmining. This had resulted in frequent use of strike action. In 1925 the mine owners cut the wages of miners. The government agreed to subsidise wages for nine months while the Samuel Commission looked at the problem. When the Commission reported and the subsidy ended, the Trades Union Congress (TUC) agreed to support the miners in a 'general strike'. However, the government was well prepared to deal with the strike. Many people, including trade unionists, were also worried about the effect of the strike on the democratic system of government. After nine days, the TUC called off the General Strike.

What do I Need to Know?

This section concentrates on one event – the General Strike of 1926. There is always likely to be a question on it somewhere in Paper 2, so it is important that you know the topic in detail. First you need to understand why the General Strike happened. There are long-term causes – the decline of British industry and poor industrial relations. These came to a head in the mining industry in 1925; the General Strike resulted from other trade unions agreeing to support the miners. Second, you will need to know why the General Strike lasted for only nine days. Here, there are a combination of reasons: the preparations of the government, the support of the media for the government, and the opposition of many people in Britain to the strike.

History of the General Strike

Reasons for the General Strike

- Trade unionists believed that strikes were the best way to bring about change. Poor industrial relations before and after the First World War had brought strikes and industrial action. The mining industry was particularly hit because export markets had been lost to new industrial nations such as Japan and the USA.
- During the First World War the government had taken over the running of coal mines. In 1921 the mines were returned to their owners.
- The mine owners reduced wages. An attempt at a general strike failed when other unions failed to support the miners (Black Friday, 15 April 1921).

- In 1925 the mine owners again tried to reduce wages and lengthen the working day. This time, other unions supported the coal miners (Red Friday, 31 July 1925).
- The government set up the Samuel Commission to look at the mining industry. During this period, the government subsidised the wages of the miners.
- The subsidy of miners' wages ended on 30 April 1926.
- The Samuel Commission failed to solve the problems. It agreed that wages should be cut, but that hours should not be lengthened. Mine owners again lowered wages, but to below the level recommended by the Commission.
- The TUC, the body representing trade unions, supported the miners and threatened a general strike.

Summary box 1

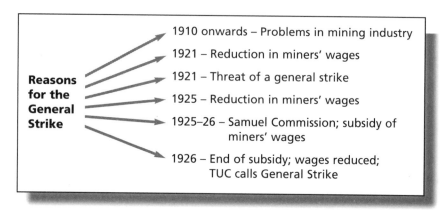

Reasons for the General Strike

- 1910 onwards – Problems in mining industry
- 1921 – Reduction in miners' wages
- 1921 – Threat of a general strike
- 1925 – Reduction in miners' wages
- 1925–26 – Samuel Commission; subsidy of miners' wages
- 1926 – End of subsidy; wages reduced; TUC calls General Strike

The General Strike: 4–12 May 1926

- 3 million workers came out on strike in support of the miners.
- Key workers, such as hospital workers, were asked not to strike.
- Essential supplies were allowed to be moved.
- In some areas of the country there was no violence, but in other areas there were clashes between strikers and non-strikers, resulting in violence and the destruction of property.
- On 12 May the General Strike was called off.

Reasons why the General Strike lasted only nine days

Organisation of the government

- The Prime Minister, Stanley Baldwin, had had a year to prepare for the General Strike. He was not prepared to give in to the TUC.
- The Organisation for the Maintenance of Supplies (OMS) was set up to make sure that key supplies such as food and power were maintained.
- The government used the armed forces to move supplies.
- The government used propaganda against the strikers. The *British Gazette,* a government newspaper, put the government's case to the British public. (The *British Worker,* the newspaper of the TUC, was not so effective.)

- The government used the BBC for radio broadcasts condemning the General Strike. The TUC could not challenge the government view of events.

Organisation of the trade unions

- The TUC had not planned for a general strike. It expected the threat of a strike would be enough to force the government to accept its terms.
- It was never a 'general' strike. Not all workers went out on strike, including many that the TUC ordered to do so.
- The TUC was divided on the purpose of the General Strike. Many trade unionists saw it as a revolution against British democracy, rather than as an industrial dispute.

Reaction of the British people to the General Strike

- Many people of all classes were against the strike as an attack on democracy.
- The middle classes in particular opposed the strike. They joined the OMS and volunteered to keep essential services running so they were able to undermine the strike.
- Volunteers drove buses and trains, unloaded ships and became special constables.
- The churches opposed the strike.
- Political parties opposed the strike – even the Labour Party.

Summary box 2

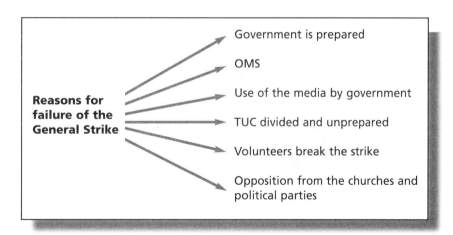

Reasons for failure of the General Strike
→ Government is prepared
→ OMS
→ Use of the media by government
→ TUC divided and unprepared
→ Volunteers break the strike
→ Opposition from the churches and political parties

Results of the General Strike

- The miners stayed out on strike until November 1926. They then returned to work on reduced wages.
- The Trade Disputes Act 1927 made a general strike illegal.
- The General Strike was a disaster for trade unions. Membership fell as workers left the unions.

4

What do I Know?

What is important about the following:

- The Samuel Commission
- The OMS?

1 Why was the mining industry in decline after the First World War?

2 What were 'Black Friday' and 'Red Friday'?

3 How did volunteers help to defeat the General Strike?

4 What kind of workers did not go on strike in 1926?

5 What was the *British Gazette*?

6 What role did the BBC play in the General Strike?

7 What did the Trade Disputes Act do?

My score ......

5

Exam Type Question

Here is the sort of source-based question you might be asked in Section A of Paper 2. It requires you to evaluate the source (7 marks) using your knowledge to support your answer (2 marks). Look closely at the answer given and the examiner's comments.

▲ Front page of the *British Gazette*, a government newspaper.

How useful is the source for learning about the General Strike? Explain your answer, using the source and your own knowledge.

(9 marks)

Answer

This source is not very useful because it is biased. It is from the British Gazette, a newspaper published by the government, so it will only give the government's point of view. You can tell that it is biased by looking at the headlines which attack the General Strike and the TUC. So we can only learn how the government felt about the General Strike.

Examiner's Comments

5 out of 9

This answer uses only the source but, as more marks are available for this, it does score quite well. If the answer had ended after the first two sentences, it would have reached only the lowest level (2 marks). However, it goes on to give examples of the limitations of the source in terms of its reliability. The final sentence also adds to the answer – the candidate is showing that, despite the bias, there is still something that we can learn about the strike. The answer would receive 5 out of the 7 marks available for evaluation. To get full marks, the candidate would need to provide knowledge to support their answer.

Practice Question

Now have a go at answering this question yourself.

Describe how the actions of the government helped to defeat the General Strike of 1926. **(5 marks)**

This is the kind of short 'free standing' knowledge question that can be found in Section B of Paper 2. It requires you to provide a short, relevant answer that shows knowledge of the issue. Note that the question asks you to deal with only one aspect of the General Strike – the actions of the government. After you have written your answer, look at the section headed 'Organisation of the government'. Have you covered all the areas mentioned there?

7.3 Britain, 1929–39: A decade of depression and recovery?

.... 1 ....

Topic Summary

In 1929 the Wall Street Crash in the USA brought economic problems across the world. Britain was one of the countries that suffered most. Unemployment rose, especially in areas of old industries – the north of England, Wales and Scotland. Here, unemployed people suffered great hardship that sometimes drove them to desperate measures – for example, the Jarrow Crusade in 1936. The government introduced a number of measures to deal with the Depression but they had only limited success. However, the picture in the 1930s was not all gloom. In the south of England new industries were established. They brought employment and prosperity to the people there.

.... 2 ....

What do I Need to Know?

You will need to look at a number of different issues. First you need to understand why Britain suffered from the Depression and to recognise how the general decline in Britain's old industries was made much worse by the effects of the Wall Street Crash in the USA. You will also need to appreciate that in the 1930s there were 'two Britains': North and South. In the north, Wales and Scotland there were many areas of high unemployment and all the problems that go with it, such as 'living on the dole' and the means test. The 'other' Britain in the south had high employment due to new industries and was much more prosperous. You will need to know what measures the government took to ease the Depression and how successful they were. And although there was some improvement, it is important to remember that it was the Second World War that ended the Depression and unemployment.

.... 3 ....

History of Britain, 1929–39

Reasons for the Depression

Decline of the old industries

Old industries such as coalmining, textiles, shipbuilding and iron and steel had been in decline throughout the 1920s:

- They had out-of-date machinery that made them inefficient, but the owners of these industries could not afford to invest in new equipment.
- They began to lose export markets to other countries whose goods were of higher quality and cheaper.

Wall Street Crash, 1929

The Wall Street Crash made things much worse – not only for Britain, but for other European countries. (If you have studied Germany during this time, you will know the effects there.)

- The USA recalled its loans from Britain.
- The USA could no longer afford to buy British goods.
- As a result, British industries began to close down and unemployment grew.

Results of the Depression

Poor north?

The old industries in decline tended to be based in particular parts of Britain: the north, Wales and Scotland. Here the Depression hit hard:

- Unemployment was high. In some towns in south Wales and the North East, six out of every ten men were unemployed.
- Where unemployment was high the whole community suffered. Shops closed because people did not have the money to buy goods. So more people became unemployed.
- Although unemployed workers received 'the dole' (unemployment benefit), this was reduced by 10 per cent in the government cuts of 1929.
- Unemployment benefit was also subject to a means test where anyone claiming benefit had to prove that they needed it. They had to declare other earnings in the family and even the value of goods in the house.
- The Jarrow Crusade is a good example of the problems caused by the Depression. In 1930 Jarrow colliery closed; then in 1931 the steel works shut down. Finally, in 1934, the local shipyard closed and most of the town's workers lost their jobs. In 1936 workers from Jarrow marched to London to ask the government to find them work. The Crusade received great support in the towns it passed through and much sympathy from the British people – but few jobs resulted from the march.
- Many men had to wait until the economy picked up again, when Britain began to rearm for war, before they found new jobs.

Summary box 1

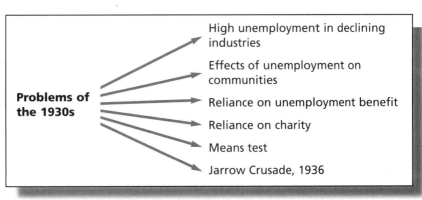

Rich south?

Higher employment encouraged many businesses to move south to be nearer their customers. In London, the South East and the Midlands, new industries were set up to produce consumer goods such as motor cars, radios and washing machines. These used modern sources of power such as electricity, modern mass-production methods and modern transport systems such as railways. In this part of Britain there was prosperity:

- Employment was high. Over nine out of every ten men had jobs.
- Employment brought a regular wage that could be used to buy consumer goods.
- Where employment was high the whole community benefited. New shops opened, including chain stores like Woolworth's and Marks & Spencer. Living standards improved.
- During the 1930s, 4 million new houses were built. This created more jobs.

Summary box 2

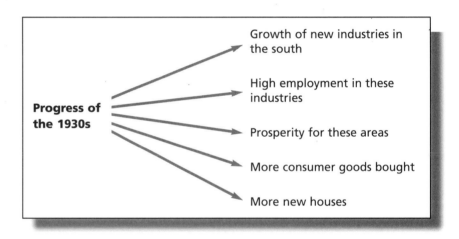

Government policies to deal with the Depression

As unemployment and the number of people claiming benefit rose in Britain, the government was spending more money than it was raising in taxes. The government had to make savings:

- **Spending cuts.** All public spending was reduced. This meant pay reductions for people such as teachers and judges – and also a 10 per cent cut in unemployment benefit.
- **A means test was introduced.** The unemployed had to reveal to local officials what every person in the household was earning and what they had in savings. The test also looked at people's belongings to see what could be sold to raise money. Children in work were expected to look after parents who were without work. Many found the means test unfair and degrading.

The government also introduced:

- **The Import Duties Act 1932.** This placed duties (taxes) on goods from abroad to make British goods cheaper. It was hoped that British people would then buy British goods and more people could be employed to make them. This worked for new industries but was much less successful in the old industries.
- **The Special Areas Act 1934.** This provided government incentives to attract new industries to old industrial areas. There were some successes, such as the Team Valley Estate in Gateshead, but new companies tended to be smaller and so employed far fewer workers than the old industries.

These actions by the government had only a limited effect in improving the economy. The approach of the Second World War, with the rearmament programme of 1937, was what really ended the Depression.

Summary box 3

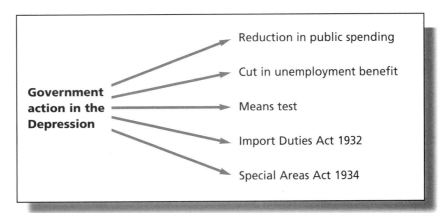

4

What do I Know?

1 Name two industries in decline in Britain between the wars.

2 Name two new industries that grew between the wars.

3 Which areas suffered most from unemployment in the 1930s?

4 Where were the new industries situated?

5 Why did the government reduce unemployment benefit by 10 per cent in 1931?

6 What did the Import Duties Act of 1932 try to do?

7 What did the Special Areas Act of 1934 try to do?

8 What finally ended the Depression in Britain?

My score ......

What is important about the following:

- The means test
- The Jarrow Crusade?

5

Exam Type Question

Here is the sort of source-based question that can be found in Section B of Paper 2. 5 marks are awarded for knowledge and 2 marks for using the evidence in the source. Look closely at the answer given and the examiner's comments.

▲ Britain during the 1930s.

Use the source and your own knowledge to explain why some areas of Britain suffered from the Depression more than others in the 1930s. **(7 marks)**

Answer

The source shows that some areas of Britain had heavy unemployment. They were the areas in England, Scotland and Wales where old industries like coalmining, iron and shipbuilding were found. In Jarrow, for example, the shipyard closed down and most of the workers there lost their jobs. Other areas of Britain suffered much less from the Depression.

Examiner's Comments

4 out of 7

This is a sound answer but there are areas for improvement. The first sentence makes the link between the Depression and unemployment. The answer then provides knowledge to link the old industries with unemployment in a general way. The use of a specific example – Jarrow – is good. The final sentence is too vague. This is the area where extra marks could have been gained.

Now see if you can provide more detailed knowledge to gain the extra marks.

6

Practice Question

I was in a transport café on the Great North Road when a young couple came in with a child. They were walking over 300 miles from South Shields near Newcastle to London because they thought he could get a job there. The baby's feeding bottle only had water in it. The baby had a newspaper nappy on.

▲ Frank Cousins, a trade union leader in the 1960s, remembers the 1930s.

Explain what you can learn from the source about the effects of the Depression of the 1930s in the North of England. **(5 marks)**

This is the kind of question that can be found in Section A of Paper 2. It requires you to examine a source and draw conclusions from that source. No additional knowledge is needed and your answer should cover only what is in the source.

7.4 Britain, 1944–51: A Changed Society?

1

Topic Summary

In 1945 a Labour government was elected to power. There was much to be done: the poverty of the 1930s remained and, in addition, Britain had suffered the effects of six years of war. The government put the Beveridge Report (1942) into operation by introducing a number of important reforms that extended the Welfare State. The reforms covered National Insurance, a National Health Service (NHS), education and housing. The Labour government also introduced state control of key industries in a policy of nationalisation. By the time the government left office in 1951, all the major industries, power supplies and transport had been nationalised.

2

What do I Need to Know?

This can be a difficult area of study because you need to know a lot of detailed information. The most important part is probably the development of the Welfare State. A good starting point is an awareness of the Beveridge Report and its main recommendations. From that you will need to know in detail the measures taken by the Labour government to deal with the five 'giant' problems identified by Beveridge. The measures that extended the Welfare State were in National Insurance and the National Health Service; but there were also other, important reforms in education and housing. Finally, you will need to understand how the Labour government extended state control to much of British industry, and you should also be able to give examples of nationalised industries.

3

History of Britain, 1944–51

The Welfare State

The Liberal government of 1905–16 had created the Welfare State (see Section 7.1). The Labour government of 1945 to 1951 extended it further, ensuring that the state helped and supported people 'from the cradle to the grave'. The government put into action many of the proposals of the Beveridge Report of 1942.

Summary box 1

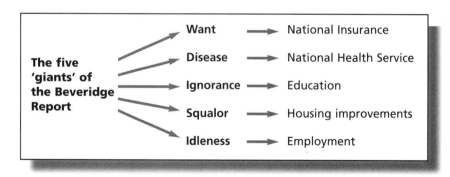

The five 'giants' of the Beveridge Report

Want → National Insurance
Disease → National Health Service
Ignorance → Education
Squalor → Housing improvements
Idleness → Employment

The attack on want: National Insurance

- Family Allowance for all families was introduced in 1946. A family would receive 5 shillings (25p) a week for each child until the child reached 16. It was a 'universal benefit' (it was given to all families).
- The National Insurance Act 1946 extended the Liberal scheme (see Section 7.1) by providing benefits to those out of work through illness, unemployment or pregnancy. As before, this was a contributory scheme into which workers, employers and the state all paid contributions. Sickness benefit had no time limit; unemployment benefit could last for six months.
- The National Insurance (Industrial Injuries) Act 1946 gave benefits to workers who were injured or disabled at work.
- The National Assistance Act 1948 set up the National Assistance Board to provide additional help for the very poor. This provided everyone with a minimum income.

Summary box 2

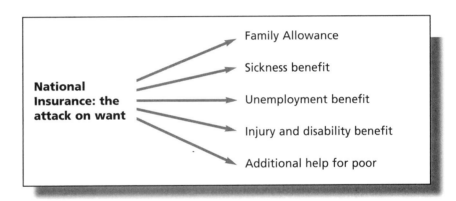

The attack on disease: the National Health Service

Aneurin Bevan, the Minister for Health, was responsible for the National Health Service Act of 1946. The new NHS began in July 1948:

- Free medical, dental, hospital and eye treatment was provided for all.
- Free medicine, spectacles and false teeth were provided for all.
- Local services like health visitors, midwives and ambulances were provided.
- Most hospitals came under NHS control.
- Doctors (GPs) were paid by the NHS. Despite some opposition from the British Medical Association (BMA), nearly all GPs joined the NHS.

The NHS was a great success. More people received treatment, and death rates from disease fell. However, the cost was far greater than had been expected. In 1951 charges were introduced on prescriptions, spectacles and dental treatment. Bevan disagreed with these charges and resigned from office.

Summary box 3

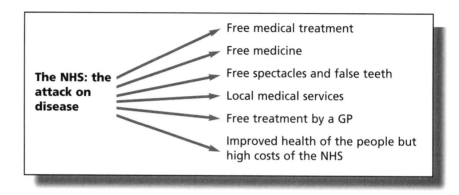

The NHS: the attack on disease
- Free medical treatment
- Free medicine
- Free spectacles and false teeth
- Local medical services
- Free treatment by a GP
- Improved health of the people but high costs of the NHS

Other reforms of the Labour government

Attack on ignorance: the Education Act 1944

The Education Act 1944 was passed before Labour came to power. The man responsible for it was a Conservative politician, R A Butler. However, it was the Labour government that put it into operation:

- It introduced free secondary education for all.
- The school leaving age was raised from 14 to 15.
- Secondary education was provided in three types of school – grammar, technical and modern. Pupils would go to the school that best suited their abilities.
- Although the three types of school were supposed to be equal, there was a greater demand for grammar school places. The 11+ exam was set up to decide which children should go to the grammar school. This meant that the secondary modern was regarded as 'second best'.

Attack on squalor: housing

There was a serious shortage of housing as a result of wartime bombing. The government took immediate action:

- Temporary accommodation was provided in 'prefabs' (prefabricated houses).
- The New Towns Act 1946 provided government money to set up new towns. It also gave grants to businesses, to attract industry to the new towns.
- New towns were built away from the large cities to reduce overcrowding. Twelve new towns were planned – most were around London but there were others in Scotland and the North East. They were carefully planned and had modern amenities.

Attack on idleness: employment

More jobs were needed:

- Marshall Aid from the USA helped industry to recover from war.
- Virtually full employment was achieved by 1950.

Nationalisation

Nationalisation means state ownership. During the Second World War the government had taken control of all important industries and transport, to ensure they met the special needs of the war. This policy was now continued by the Labour government. Its reasons for doing this were:

- The interests of the workers would be protected.
- Profits made by these industries would go to the state and not to private owners. The profits could then be used to help people in the Welfare State.
- The government would provide the money needed to modernise the industries.

(You could look at the problems in the mining industry discussed in Section 7.2 to understand these reasons better.)

Summary box 4

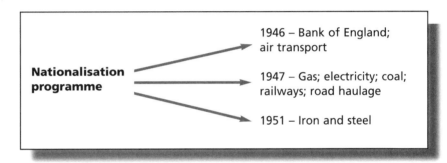

Nationalisation programme

1946 – Bank of England; air transport

1947 – Gas; electricity; coal; railways; road haulage

1951 – Iron and steel

...4

What do I Know?

What is important about the following:
- The Beveridge Report
- National Insurance
- The National Health Service?

1 Name two 'giants' attacked by Beveridge.

2 Who was insured by the National Insurance Act of 1946?

3 Who was responsible for setting up the National Health Service?

4 Name the three types of school set up in the Education Act of 1944.

5 What was a 'new town'?

6 What is meant by 'nationalisation'?

7 Name two industries that were nationalised by the Labour government.

My score ......

........5........

Exam Type Question

Here is the sort of essay question you might be asked in an exam paper. Look closely at the answer given and the examiner's comments on it. Then try to answer the question yourself in about 20 minutes.

> Did the welfare reforms introduced by the Labour Government, 1945-51, improve the conditions of life of the British people? Explain your answer. **(15 marks)**

Answer

The Labour government introduced welfare reform in two important areas - National Insurance and the National Health Service. Both improved the condition of life of people.

National Insurance covered a lot of different areas. The Act of 1946 provided insurance when people became unemployed, sick, pregnant, widowed or injured at work. There were also family allowances for every child after the first one. Old Age Pensions continued and death grants were also added to provide decent funerals. All these types of insurance meant that the promise to look after people from the cradle to the grave was kept. National Insurance was paid for by weekly contributions from every worker, every employer and the state. For the very poor there was also national assistance that brought extra benefits.

The NHS was set up in 1948. It provided free treatment by doctors, dentists, opticians and at hospital. It also provided free medicine and spectacles. Midwives and health visitors were available free of charge. All this brought a great change to people's lives. Before the NHS, people had to pay for treatment and often could not afford it. Now the services were free. There was a great rush to have treatment and the NHS became expensive to run. So the government introduced charges on things like medicines and dental treatment. This was unpopular.

The welfare reforms improved life for the people. National Insurance gave people help when they most needed it. The NHS meant that people were able to be healthier and to live longer.

Examiner's Comments

14 out of 15

This answer reaches the top level and it is worth looking at the reasons why. It covers the relevant reforms in plenty of accurate detail. The opening sentence is important – it tells us that the candidate knows exactly what is required to answer the question. The answer shows a good understanding of the question and makes a number of references to how the reforms improved the quality of life for people. It would be possible to pick out some errors or omissions – for example, injuries benefit is included in the National Insurance Act when it is a separate act. However, these are minor points when compared to the amount of accurate information contained in the answer.